SPEAK II

Nancy Bauer-King

in medias res

Speaking the Truth in Love
A Conversation

© 2023 by Nancy Bauer-King

Permission is given for copying for educational purposes by congregations and non-profits for their local purposes. Other reproduction or transmission of the contents requires the express written permission of the publisher:

in medias res

In Medias Res, LLC
1009 Quincy Street
Onalaska, WI 54650.

Note: Some names have been changed.

ISBN 978-1-7375798-5-4

Bauer-King, Nancy, 1940–
  Speaking the Truth in Love: A Conversation /
  Nancy Bauer-King

  1. Memoir /
  2. Spirituality /
  3. Grief Process /

For Charlie's children
Karen, David, and Gayle

> You start by writing to live.
> You end by writing so as not to die.
> – Carlos Fuentes

I am so grateful for the friends and family (you know who you are) who were present with me during the pandemic and through Charlie's illness and death. Throughout the writing of this book, I am grateful to the Reverend Doctor Dwight Judy, whose grace-filled listening and cogent questions helped me continue the process. I am also grateful for people who actually read my writing and encouraged me to keep on keepin' on, namely the folks in the Tuesday afternoon Round Table at Red Oak Studio. Then there is Kim Suhr, Director of Red Oak, whose writing and leadership skills, keen copy-editing eyes, and generosity are unparalleled. Kim deserves credit and a big thank you for the completion of this book. Finally, a special thank you to Brenda and Wesley White, another couple in ministry who have known me and still loved me for over fifty years. Imagine that!

Table of Contents

Speaking the Truth in Love	3
Jesus Has Double Vision	7
The Vine, Dead Wood, and Branches	8
Increase Our Faith	10
The Women Who Were Concerned	11
Galilee (Easter Sunday)	12
Is Hell a Burning Question?	13
Samson	14
Deep Listening in a Shallow World	15
David and Goliath	16
To Drink or Not to Drink	18
The Ingredients for Inner Peace	20
Snake Giving and Prayer	21
United Methodist Beliefs for Today: The Church	22
Are You Ready for Anything?	24
Holiness in Our Feelings	26
Jesus' Mission and Ours	27
War in Heaven and on Earth	29
Pray for the Living and the Dead	31
Peace and Persecution	34
Celebrate the Temporary	36
Faithfulness, Faith, and Freedom	38
Jesus Through the Eyes of the Crowd	40
Life Has Meaning	41
The Shortness of Life	42
Sing of Hope and Healing	45
Faithfulness, Faith, and Freedom	46
The Characteristics of Christians	51
Blind Samson	52
Love is Not Rude or Selfish	53
Love and Marriage	55
I Believe	57
Born of the Spirit	59
Simon of Cyrene	60
Fear and Faith	62
Invitation to Join the Barnabas Club	64
Disciples Are Called	67
Spirit, Water, and Blood	70
How to be Remembered	71
Anger: One Letter Short of Danger	73
Happy Are the Sad	75

The Surprising Advent	77
What Shall I Do With Jesus?	78
What About Life After Death?	80
Heavenly Worship	81
We Are Surrounded	84
Enter God: Into Old Age	86
Amazement	88
Our Fathers Who Are on Earth	89
Lydia	93
Stop, or Go?	95
Lent Us Pray	98
God Who?	100
The Woman Who Talked Back to Jesus	101
If You Lived in Antioch (1)	103
If You Lived in Antioch (2)	105
Jesus the Liberator	107
We Heard That God is With You	108
Avoid Murder and Lying	110
Some Dos and Don'ts When Suffering Comes (1)	111
Some Dos and Don'ts When Suffering Comes (2)	112
Some Dos and Don'ts When Suffering Comes (3)	113
Forget the Funeral	116
What Do You Mean, Salvation?	118
Christian Perfection	120
What is the Spiritual LIfe?	123
Joseph and That Coat	125
How to Know Right From Wrong	127
Playing at Religion	129
The Handwriting on the Wall	130
You Can't Keep A Secret	132
The Borrowing Christ	134
What is a Christian?	138
Making Human Relations Christian	140
Praise the Lord	144
Hope When the World Changes	146
A Letter to Cody	149
Expect Joy	152
The Scandal of the Cross	156
Wrestling With God	158
Until Death Do Us Part	161
Speaking the Truth in Love	164

December 1, 2022

Dear Charlie,

    This morning's front-page headline in the *Racine Journal Times*—**A Witness To History Brought Down**—grabbed my attention. The article with an accompanying photo recounted the demise of the burr oak tree on the lawn of First United Methodist Church in Kenosha. Called a landmark, the oak was estimated to be 248 years old. The article mentioned several changes the tree had seen in the city over its decades of life.

    Charlie, my love, the old oak also *witnessed* you going in and out of that church almost every day for eleven years. And you and me. How many times did we stop on our way into a potluck or concert or strawberry festival just to look at that staunch sentinel's sturdy branches stretching out over the lawn?

    You were 84 when you died. Strangely enough, you died in Burr Oak, a care facility in Genoa City. You were not a landmark, but you were a strong and steady life-long pastor who witnessed countless changes in the world, nation, and United Methodist Church. Of more importance were the changes in the people you served and knew and loved.

    Including me.

    Those first few days after your death, I was wracked with sobs, flooded with papers to sign and bills to pay. I replayed haunting memories of the last four months of your life. Phone calls, emails, cards from children and friends kept me from drowning. But, because of the pandemic there was no funeral for you. No formal celebration of who you were. Your gifts. Your personality. Your quirks. No place where people could express their love for you.

    Or me.

    Twelve days after you died, a hospice grief counselor called. She introduced herself and asked, "How are you?"

"I'm a mess."
"What do you mean?"
"I cry a lot."
(silence)
"Are you eating?"
"Yes."
"Hydrating?"
"Yes."
"Do you have a friend?"
"Yes."
"What is the hardest thing for you right now?"
"*Not being able to be with Charlie for the past four months of his life.*"

The counselor seemed to sympathize with the situation I had faced—your advanced dementia, Covid-19 prohibiting my visits to you in the Memory Care units, support of family and friends only by phone or email.

Then, she suggested, "You could try writing letters to Charlie."

I thought of all the times I had proposed this very idea to folks in relationship pain. "He won't answer."

"You could respond in the words of the Charlie you knew."

Charlie, initially, I dismissed her idea—someone *else's* idea—of what *I* could do. Later, I tried her suggestion. Not knowing where you were and not trusting in any answers from you, I achingly and tearfully filled three-fourths of a leather notebook.

You didn't answer.

Were you watching? *Witnessing?*

If so, you would have seen me contact Dwight, the man with whom in the late 1990s, I completed certification for spiritual guidance. Somewhere in my biweekly zoom conversations with Dwight, I had an idea—*my* idea.

I began to read through two large cardboard cartons of your sermons, half of which you preached years before I knew you. Surprisingly, after a few pages, you came alive again through your words. I began to talk with you. Laugh. Cry. Argue. Give you updates. I saved a few dozen sermons to which I had strong reactions and began a conversation with you that lasted a year and a half.

Like the burr oak, these pages are a witness to the caring and faith-filled man you were, a testament to the love you shared with me.

This morning I said, "Charlie, do you think it would be okay to have these conversations published?"

You laughed and answered, "Well, when did you ever ask my permission to do something you *wanted* to do?"

Pretty much, never.

Speaking the Truth in Love
Ephesians 4.1–16
First UMC, Appleton (1/31/1982)

[Charlie]

My first memories of this church take me back to my seminary days when, as assistant minister at First Church West Allis, I came to Pastor's School at Appleton. Standing here where I am right now was the tall, grey-haired impressive figure of Bishop Northcott. There was also another minister up front, and though he didn't have as much hair on his head as Bishop Northcott, I'm glad this didn't disqualify Ralph Alton from becoming bishop. Since that time, I have known all the pastors who have served this congregation. I have known some better than others, of course, but that knowledge leaves me with an awareness of the great cloud of witnesses who have gone before. And it is scary!

Shortly after I met with your Pastor Parish Relations Committee, I found this definition in a magazine I was reading: "Anxiety is the normal emotional response to anything new, unexpected, and uncharted." I got out my magic marker, wrote down the definition, and put it above my desk (in Oconomowoc). And I brought it here and put it up, too.

Anxiety. You have it this morning to some degree as you sit there and wonder what kind of pastor, preacher, teacher, administrator, prophet, parent, and husband this Charles King is. And my anxiety arising from the new and the uncharted that lies before us is mixed with sadness and grief at leaving hundreds of people in Oconomowoc whom I loved and for whom I cared deeply. But there is also the joy of new growth, new adventures in which we will share, the joy of new friendships, and the entrance into a new and exciting community of caring and committed Christians ...

Well, we'll learn a lot about each other in the years that lie ahead. For now, let me mention just a few things which will guide me in my ministry among you ...

... Someone has said, "If we are not enjoying our religion, something must be wrong with it." I agree. We have gathered to celebrate life. So in what we do here in worship and what we do out there, let us express the joy and excitement of a people who have been challenged by Christ the Disturber, who have been restored by Christ the Healer, and who have made a commitment to Christ the Lord and Master.

I pledge to you my commitment *always* to speak the truth as I understand the truth; and I will always *try* to speak the truth in a spirit of love, that together we may grow up in every way to Christ, who is our head.

[Nancy]

Charlie, today is November 22, 2022. For a year and a half I have been reading, sorting, and writing responses to some of the sermons you preached over 60 years of ministry. The circumstances of your death two years ago were wrenching. My responses to your sermons became a way to be in touch with you as well as to recover much of your life in the years before the shroud of dementia fell over you.

In my initial sorting, I found five "Speaking the Truth in Love" sermons, each one using the scripture from Ephesians. You preached this topic on the first Sunday you arrived at a new appointment and then again as you departed that congregation. Though each sermon consists of the same general outline, details differ depending upon the occasion and the congregation.

Early in this process, I set all five aside, thinking they might provide a good ending piece for the collection, but yesterday, contrary to a statement attributed to Jesus, "the last will be first and the first, last" (Matthew 20.16), I've decided one of these firsts will be first and one of the lasts last.

I'm choosing this sermon because you preached it on the first Sunday you began to serve First United Methodist Church in Appleton and your arrival there coincided with your arrival into my life.

Do you remember the day we met? The pastor of the church I attended, drove me to First Church to meet you. I had indicated an interest in ordained ministry and needed to complete a six-session "Inquiring Candidate" process with someone who had the necessary certification to lead. You'd already mentored several future pastors, so you obviously knew what you were doing.

    Your office door was open when we arrived. You stood from behind your desk, shook my hand, and after a short conversation suggested that we make an appointment to get better acquainted and then decide whether or not to pursue the candidacy process. I was anxious. I didn't want you. You seemed fake. Too effusive. Too happy. But you were the only available choice.

    I remember lugging around that royal blue three-ring binder with page after page outlining a process to *explore* professional UMC ministry. I had no clue about the books, papers, classes, and subsequent 30+ steps I would need to complete in the next three years. Except for the time you stifled a yawn (I was boring?) and the meeting we had after a chaplain told me I wouldn't make a good pastor, other recollections are lost.

    When you gave me a copy of the signed recommendation you sent to the Board of Ordained Ministry for my continuance, I sighed with relief and put the heavy binder on a closet shelf.

    I entered Garrett-Evangelical Theological Seminary that fall, hoping to learn more about my religion. Maybe even enjoy it.

Jesus Has Double Vision
Luke 19.1–10
Immanuel UMC, Kenosha (11/4/2001)
Little Prairie UMC (10/31/2004)

[Charlie]

... I had about a dozen or so district superintendents as my supervisors in my forty plus years as a United Methodist pastor. Nearly all of them were quite willing to talk with me when I called them about a problem or an issue, but only two out of the twelve ever took the initiative and called me just to find out how things were going for me.

"How is it with your soul?" My District Superintendent would ask me about every six months. She took the initiative in seeking to know about me and establishing and then maintaining a relationship. And in doing so she was modeling the caring ministry of Jesus—Jesus who initiates the conversation with Zacchaeus, the tax collector: "Zacchaeus, hurry up and come down, for I must stay at your house today." And he came sliding down so fast that, as legend has it, he knocked some bark off the tree—and to this day you can see white splotches on the trunk of sycamore trees.

... Jesus was one who could always "see double." He not only sees what we are, but what we might become—our potential. He is not concerned primarily for what Zacchaeus or you or I have been, or even what we are right now. He sees in us what God intended us to become!

[Nancy]

Yes. I remember our D.S. asking me how my soul was. I was in my first year in ministry. 1985. I don't know what I answered. She talked with me a bit about the divorce I was going through. And, later, she questioned my relationship with you.

"We are good friends," I said.

Early in the Methodist movement, John Wesley, a founder, asked each participant in the small weekly meetings he led, "How is it with your soul?" Two weeks ago, while facilitating a group on Wesley's organizational genius, I tried the question on the folks. Nobody answered. We did, however, end up in a great discussion about the definition of soul.

So last week I tried the same question with different words. "How is it going in your relationship with God?" This time the ensuing discussion was the definition of God. Again, a wide continuum of images was shared.

Of course, to answer these questions means rendering oneself vulnerable. But these people knew each other well, shared life's ups and downs, took soup to folks healing from surgery, and without questioning accepted each other's take on the Holy.

No one asked how it was with my soul. Ultimately, "It is well with my soul" as the hymn refrain claims. But I am grieving your death and I have been unsuccessful in writing a poem about the swing at Lutz Park.

The Vine, Dead Wood, and Branches
John 15.1–17
Native American Ministry (5/25/2003)
Calvary UMC, Milwaukee (5/17/2009)

[Charlie]

Several years ago, Nancy ordered four lilac bushes from a nursery—each was to produce a different color flower. They are growing nicely but only one has produced any flowers—two white flowers. And of this morning there were buds forming only on that one bush. Nancy's attitude, "Let's cut them down!" My attitude: "Let's give them another year."

... Now I'm not prone to talk a lot about judgment and punishment because I think the misuse of threats and fear by many over the years has been abominable and blinds people to God's grace. Nevertheless, when we repeatedly ignore the danger signals and warnings *perhaps* God says, "No more warnings. You are simply not bearing fruit; you appear to have closed yourself off from the living vine that gives you life."

[Nancy]

God "who?" Which god are you talking about? For thirty years your image of the Holy stayed the same. How did you do that? Of course, your illustration referred to Jesus' saying, "I am the vine and you are the branches." You preached if one is separated from the Vine Jesus, the result is dead wood that needs to be chopped down.

What about all my questions about Jesus? My heresies? My questioning his virgin birth, his dying for me, his bodily resurrection? I notice that in your illustration, you were the one that didn't want to cut down the lilac bushes.

Anyway, it's not Jesus I'm thinking of with your lilac illustration. I'm thinking of the lilacs you brought me the day of my divorce. The lavender and white lilacs you found in the cemetery off Richmond Street. The stems cut with the jackknife you kept in your right pants pocket. I buried my face into the sweet, sweet scent of those lilacs. Each spring thereafter you brought me lilacs.

I don't know what staying close to Jesus means. I do know that being cut off from you during those last four months of your life was an anguishing severance.

Increase Our Faith
Luke 17.1–6
First UMC, Kenosha (7/18/1999)

[Charlie]

... I know that the day-by-day experiences in *my* life trying to follow the Christ are a series of ups and downs. And, I realize there will always be a gap between what I am and what I know I *can* be. There will always be that knowledge that my faith could be stronger than it is and that there are things I do and attitudes I hold that hinder the receiving of God's gift of faith and power. And, my guess is that that's true for you as well. Right?

Thomas Merton once wrote,

When the time comes to enter the darkness in which we are helpless and alone; in which we see the insufficiency of our greatest strength and hollowness of our strongest virtues; in which we have nothing on our own to rely on and nothing in our nature to support us, and nothing in the world to guide us or give us light—then we find out whether or not we live by faith.

[Nancy]

What happened to you in those Memory Care places, sweetie? I imagine your experience of dementia was the first time in your life you entered the darkness Merton talked about. Swallowed up in it. Alone. And, because of Covid-19, I was not allowed in to support you. I cry. No one would let me in any of those places to be with you. By the time you were moved from Azura, you didn't know who I was. Did you have something or someone to hang onto?

I reread your sermon. Ever the practical pastor, you talked about being a disciple as an ongoing adventure. You listed four suggestions for continuing to develop a mature faith. One of those suggestions was to use guilt as an opportunity for growth.

My remembrances of your last four months are saturated with guilt. I'm considering your suggestion.

The Women Who Were Concerned
Luke 10.38–42
First UMC, Kenosha (7/15/1990)

[Charlie]

Getting married and merging two households after several years of independent living has been an interesting experience for me, to say the least. Nancy and I are trying to use the words "our" and "ours" to refer to things, but often we still think in terms of "my" and "mine." My room, my couch, my mayonnaise, etc. Among the things brought into the marriage by Nancy are nearly six years of sermons. Four years ago, she preached a sermon on this text of the morning. It's good!

And so I want to start today's message by reading the beginning of a—"*our*"—four-year-old sermon.

[Nancy]

What a surprise to find this, Charlie! I remember the Mary and Martha sermon.

You read the whole first page ... how I knew exactly what happened as Martha prepared for Jesus and company: hunting frantically for her mother's famous chicken recipe; ordering new pillows to spruce up the shabby couch; painting the chipped newel post; making her brother, Lazarus, pull out the refrigerator so she could vacuum the year's dust behind it ...

I'm laughing all over again.

Then you referred to a sermon you had preached on this text eleven years earlier—how you really lit into Martha and were judgmental about her busyness. Your confession indicated a softening of your judgmentalism. The rest of your sermon moved into issues of family dynamics. You were kind to both Mary and Martha.

We were six weeks into a new marriage when you preached this and struggling with our own communication issues.

Galilee (Easter Sunday)
Matthew 28.1–10
First UMC, Kenosha   (4/12/1998)

[Charlie]

The resurrection is the answer to a real question: "Is that all there is?" The Gospels do not *explain* the resurrection. The resurrection *explains* the Gospels ... why they were written. Belief in the resurrection is not an appendage to the Christian faith. It *is* the Christian faith.

[Nancy]

How on earth did we ever make it through thirty years? More to the point—what did you think about *my* take on the resurrection? I cannot believe that I will come back to life as Nancy after I've been pronounced dead. Where I was before I was born and where I will be after I'm dead is a complete mystery over which I have no control.

And I don't know where you are now, my love. But as I go through these sermons, I can hear your voice. I can see you behind the pulpit in your white robe and colorful Bolivian stole. What does this mean? Am I charged with bringing you alive? Resurrecting you?

Is Hell a Burning Question?
John 3.16–21; 1 Timothy 2.1–4
First UMC, Kenosha (11/20/94)

[Charlie]
Perhaps at this point it's time to share with you my understanding of this burning question. For one thing, I believe that hell is people determining their own way of life. *The Book of Acts* says that Judas turned aside from discipleship "to go to his own place." In other words, he cut himself completely off from the influence of his Master and followed the bent of his own nature.

… Thus, judgment is not so much *God's* sentence upon us as it is our *own* choice. We bring it on ourselves. … As one scholar put it, "to go to hell is to be cut off from the true God because we have preferred to remain with gods of our own making." Let's think of hell less as a place and more as the heart's disposition and orientation.

[Nancy]
We may not have agreed on an afterlife, but we definitely agreed on the theology of hell, didn't we? Neither of us believed in an afterlife with gnashing of teeth. Hell for me was right here on earth while I was separated from you.

I'm irritated you are still referring to Jesus as Master. Even after I told you several times how much I hate that word. Dredges up images of slavery. And a more powerful male in charge of me. You listened to my ranting and once in a while used other names. While I spent years vacillating in my belief, you never wavered.

Samson
Judges 13–16 (selected)
First UMC, Kenosha (7/6/1997)

[Charlie]

At one of our church meetings a couple months ago, I told of my preaching plans for the summer—sermons based on some of the familiar Old Testament stories taught to us in Sunday School. When I finished one of our members commented, "You didn't mention any stories about women in your plans."

"Well," I responded with defensiveness, "There's Samson and Delilah." I knew that wasn't a satisfactory answer, but it got the laugh I expected. However, my wife didn't laugh when I told her about the incident…

[Nancy]

No. I didn't laugh. You knew how sensitive I was about Biblical women. Except for Jael who drove a tent stake through Sisera's head, the women are either virgins, mothers, or whores.

And, of course, widows. Ruth, Naomi, and the poor unnamed woman in Jesus' story about giving. Widows are ubiquitous throughout the scriptures and along with orphans are supposed to be taken care of.

Widow. I don't like the word. I don't know what being a widow means. I'm trying to learn.

You did include Delilah in that sermon. To your credit, you acknowledged she was probably a Philistine and added that if the Philistines were telling this story she would have been a heroine. I'd like to hear a Delilah Heroine story.

Deep Listening in a Shallow World
Psalm 81.1–3, 8–13; James 1.19–21
First UMC, Kenosha (7/4/1999)

[Charlie]

Many years ago, when I was pastor of the English-speaking church in La Paz, Bolivia, I had the opportunity to attend quite a few dinners and parties at both the American and the British embassies. One time I was trying to set up a meeting with a church member after one of these American Embassy parties. Well, he was unable to meet with me then and that's when I learned that after *all* the get-togethers, the diplomats and staff were expected to return to the American Embassy for debriefing. It was a time for them to respond to Ambassador Henderson's question: "What did you hear tonight?" For them the dinners and parties were work and a part of their work was to listen and report.

It *is* work to listen—hard work sometimes.

I'm still learning to listen … My wife comes home from a meeting at her church frustrated and disappointed, perhaps angry and irritated. And, as she describes what transpired, I see, almost instantly, four or five solutions, approaches, possibilities. I'm ready to offer her file folders filled with information. If on occasion, you see teeth marks on my lips, they are self-inflicted, by me biting my lip in an attempt to keep my mouth shut and listen. As a pastoral counselor I've learned to go sparingly with the advice. As a husband, I'm still working at it!

[Nancy]

Working at it, Charlie? I had to teach you! We'd been married nine years when you preached that sermon and you were finally catching on that I just needed to blurt out my distress. I was 59 and still fighting to find my own answers—what *I* needed, not what someone else with more power decided I needed. Naturally, as a woman I was conditioned to be subordinate and for way too long thought I needed a strong male to solve all my problems. Did you find strength through listening?

I prided myself as a good listener, too, until you began fading into dementia and asking me the same question over and over within three minutes. I had no clue what you were feeling and you couldn't tell me.

I am so sorry.

David and Goliath
1 Samuel 17 (portions)
First UMC, Kenosha (7/13/1997)

[Charlie]

... I've seen slingshots like that used by David in the hands of Bolivian children—girls and boys.

As in David's time, the children are often left with the sheep and they use their slings—a woven rope with a loop on one end that slips over the small finger, a wide section in the middle where the stone is placed, and then the remaining cord which is held between the thumb and forefinger while the sling is twirled in the air just prior to releasing it. The children use their slings to control the sheep.

[Nancy]
You describe your experiences in Bolivia more often than any other personal reflections. I know how formative your ministry was in La Paz, but you rarely mentioned children other than your own. Where did you see these children? Were they in your church or in your classes at the Methodist American Institute?

I saw how children loved you, how you engaged with them immediately whenever they showed up in your presence. You knelt down to be at their level. Showed them tricks with your fingers. Sometimes you asked them if they liked to swing. If they nodded, you bent over, laced the fingers of your hands together, making a swing out of your outstretched arms. Young children crawled into them, leaned their heads against your chest and giggled as you cradled them back and forth.

I remember your steady arms swinging me through our dance lessons with the chubby middle-aged teacher whose toes squeezed between the thin black straps on her pumps as she demonstrated steps to the Oakridge Boys "Elvira."

I dream that you are sitting on the swing in Lutz Park. You are in your light gray suit, white shirt, and lighthouse tie. You are turned away from the river toward the hill, your left arm is resting on the back of the swing. You are watching for me to arrive.

To Drink or Not to Drink
Romans 14.13–17, 19, 21; 15.1–2;
1 Corinthians 6.12
First UMC, Appleton (1/17/1988)

[Charlie]

To drink or not to drink? A sermon on alcohol is usually preached to a congregation in which there are divided opinions. For some the issue is quite clear. In our Methodist heritage total abstinence was expected of every member. In fact, prior to ordination, clergy took a vow of abstinence, and, until 1964 no one who drank any alcoholic beverages was supposed to be elected to any church office or committee.

… Obviously, then, there was a lot of hypocrisy around this drinking issue. I know that years ago, on several occasions, I was left standing outside members' homes while the bottles and glasses were hastily rushed out to the kitchen; then I entered and we all played the game of pretending that everything was as it was "supposed" to be in the good Methodist homes.

And there remains a lot of hypocrisy, guilt, deception, and confusion. Several years ago, a group of clergy and laity were eating and drinking at Karras' restaurant and another pastor who was with us asked for his wine to be served in a coffee cup lest members of his congregation enter and see him drinking wine.

… Let's spend our remaining time today building a base upon which all Christians can stand and make some decisions, without getting all hung up on this emotional wet/dry, abstinence/moderation issue …

[Nancy]

Ah, sweetheart, for the first page and a half of this sermon you present facts and statistics. You sounded just like my father who carried temperance literature in his shirt pocket, carefully cut out every alcohol related automobile accident from the Janesville *Gazette*, and convinced me that if I ever took a first drink, my brain would atrophy into the size of a walnut, and I would die on Skid Row clutching a bottle to my chest.

I read your whole sermon. You do not name the church member who requested that you preach on this subject—a member who was probably more interested in hearing if you imbibed than all the rest of your message. And, in this eight-page exhortation, you don't reveal that you've broken that old vow.

You've read the story of my first taste of alcohol—champagne at the neighbors the afternoon Ginny found out her P.O.W. husband who had been shot down over Viet Nam six years earlier, was alive. How could I not celebrate? I was 33.

You? Wasn't your first drink in some restaurant while you were in seminary? Was that when you discovered wine tasted like vinegar in your mouth? What a gift to me! Me, who was trying to make up for lost time and you, a built-in designated driver.

Well, in this sermon, after you list the dire facts, read the scripture, (in which wine is a blessing), relate a couple anecdotes, and share your work as an alcohol treatment counselor, you list issues for folks to consider regarding their use of alcohol.

No judgments. Only issues. And you conclude with Paul's statement, "Whether you eat or drink, or whatever you do, do all to the glory of God."

Charlie. Remember the night at the bar when you tied the stem of the cherry from your drink into a knot using only your tongue? I'm not sure about God, but I loved it!

The Ingredients for Inner Peace
Psalm 46.1–7; Philippians 4.5–9
First UMC, Appleton (4/8/1984)

[Charlie]
    Peace is one of those commonly used words that carries a number of meanings and images. On Friday, Dave, Nancy, and I attended a workshop at St. Mary's Medical Center in Madison. In the course of that experience, we were led through a number of exercises in imaging, picturing scenes both past and present in our minds' eyes.

    That led me to wonder; what kinds of images do you have when I speak of inner peace, peace of mind, peacefulness? What do you think of when you hear Jesus saying, "My peace I give you ..." or when Paul talks about the "peace which passes understanding," or about "letting the peace of God rule in your hearts ..."?

    Close your eyes and try to formulate a picture of peace in your mind right now.

    ... Where was the scene? In a woods, along a river or lake, looking up at the stars or out at a sunrise?

[Nancy]
    What scene did you see then, Charlie? Somewhere in Bolivia? For several years after our marriage, you reported dreams of Bolivia and how you missed being there. Were your dream images peaceful? In the last four years of your life, you seemed to be at peace looking out at the lake from the blue leather recliner.

    That Friday workshop? I was in my second year of seminary. You and Dave were supervising my Field Ed placement. I had been doing guided imagery and meditation for several years and talked both of you skeptics into attending. In spite of all your teasing, your sermon indicates you got something out of the experience to share with the congregation.

Now, when I follow your invitation to close my eyes and think of peace, I'm sitting on the swing with you at Lutz Park. You have suggested taking a break from the demands of the office to share with me the year-end evaluation of my Field Ed work. I do not remember the evaluation. I do remember sipping coffee and watching the ducks play hide and seek amidst the reeds at the edge of the Fox River.

I do not know I am falling in love with you.

Snake Giving and Prayer
Psalm 52; Luke 11.1–13
Immanuel UMC, Kenosha (7/22/2001)
Little Prairie UMC (7/25/2004)

[Charlie]
God's love! I was a part of a worship service in Washington, D.C. three years ago in which the worship leader told the five hundred of us there to greet one another; but instead of saying "Hello" or "Peace be with you," we were to say, "God loves you and there's nothing you can do about it."

I thought that was a wonderful greeting. It's a reminder of God's grace!

[Nancy]
Eeew! I think that is a *terrible* greeting. To me the words are intrusive and evoke my feelings of powerlessness. Though the theology (Christian) *may* be accurate, I'm glad I wasn't at that service because I couldn't have played that leader's game.

And you? In all our loving words, did we ever pull rank on each other?

Your sermon was about unanswered prayer and Jesus' promise to his disciples in Luke. Jesus says (in red letters in my Bible), "…the heavenly Father will give the Holy Spirit to those who *ask* …"

Did you get a chance to *ask* for God's love before it was foisted upon you?

My prayer is to the god—whatever god it is—that will keep me away from worship leaders like the one in DC and others of their ilk.

United Methodist Beliefs for Today: The Church
Ephesians 2.17–22, 4.1–6, 15–16
First UMC, Appleton (3/4/1984)

[Charlie]

Two weeks ago, the fourteen of us who were in Mexico worshipped with a congregation of Mexican Methodists. It was a high point in our experience and we referred to that worship time quite a bit during the days that followed. Naturally, there were comparisons made between that church service and our own. Granted that our feelings were based on just one visit; and granted that other Mexican Methodist Church services might not be like that one. In fact, one that I attended seven years before was deadly. Nevertheless, I think what moved us was the fact that many of those worshippers were first-and-second generation Christians who were filled with an enthusiasm for their faith that was rooted in Christ. Ours is more likely to be a cut-flower faith without roots.

[Nancy]
Yup. I see myself as a cut-flower Christian. Maybe a red rose in a three-day old arrangement with its drying petals dropping on the white countertop like fat blobs of blood.

Before describing your experience with the Mexican Church, you spent five pages of this sermon describing the Christian church in the U.S. You ended by inviting the congregation to join in a responsive creed.

But, like your description of a first-generation Christian, you never lost your enthusiasm.

You woke up happy every morning. You stayed energetic and *up* through most of the days. Only rarely did you seem *down* and your funk didn't last long.

Me. I wake up cranky and thirty years ago was diagnosed chronically depressed by some Mayo Clinic doc who spent three minutes with me.

I still believe him.

Anyway, I would rather swim naked through an alligator infested swamp than go on another mission trip.

We'd been married about a year when you talked me into co-leading a journey to some church camp outside of Louisville. Twelve of us piled into two vans and after seven hours on the road, we spent a week in sweltering heat painting a few buildings some god-awful puke green color.

My grandson, John, had died a few months earlier. I was losing all my hair. Even my eyebrows. Everything hurt. And I don't remember a single rousing worship service with the staff at that camp.

Did they even thank us?

I never went on another mission trip, but you kept going. Massachusetts, Arkansas, Mexico, Cuba, Guyana, Bolivia. Dozens of trips. All over the world.

Are You Ready for Anything?
Philippians 1.21–23; 4.12–23
First UMC, Appleton (4/22/84)

[Charlie]

... On Easter Sunday seventeen years ago, I started my sermon with a statement that caused several people such anxiety and anger that they never returned to that church again. I didn't learn until a long time later that my opening sentences had had that effect.

Do you know what I said?

"Before next Easter, at least two of you who are sitting here now will be dead. These are the statistical facts! Are you willing to accept them?"

Then I went on to affirm the Christian faith in the resurrection of the body and life everlasting. But some people were so threatened by the fact of their own mortality or the possible loss of a loved one that they apparently heard not another word.

But I'm a little older and wiser and realize that so often faith breaks down at this very point. Faith has been sufficient for life, but it does not seem to be sufficient for death. It's not "the strife is o'er, the battle won..." It's rather, "the strife is o'er, the battle lost." So, I would never start off an Easter sermon talking about the possibility of death for any of us. I might be tempted to bring in that fact about fifteen minutes into the message, but then immediately hasten to say this: here's the secret of victory over death and anxiety about death: If you and I have lived only for ourselves, our own pleasure and comfort and success and security, then death, by putting an end to those things will certainly seem to defeat us. But if we live for Christ, if his will and way have been the purpose of our lives, then death is seen, not as the final frustration, but as the entrance to new and greater opportunities. And we will be ready for it and for anything else.

Yes. Anything. All because of the strength given to us through the Risen One, Jesus.

[Nancy]

Ready for *anything*? I remember the Easter morning you preached that sermon. You and Dave decided that because the date was so late in April, the weather *had* to be good. You arranged for the Sunrise Service to be held in the Lawrence University Bowl and still trying to be a good little Field Ed student, I agreed to play the *field* organ you and Dave dragged out. That morning *none of us were ready* for the blizzard. Luckily, to thwart the snow and wind trying to whip the hymn pages into the stadium stands, I had two gripper clothespins to fasten the music to the rack of the organ, but my fingers were numbing up. So was the forced smile on my face.

Though a couple dozen intrepid congregants appeared, the sun did not and the planned half-hour service lasted about ten minutes. We didn't laugh about it until after we had hauled everything back to the church and after you preached your "Are You Ready for Anything?" sermon in a warm sanctuary.

Were you ready for your death, Charlie? You were not ready for short term memory loss. Several times we talked and cried. Several times you said, "I will get better."

"No. You will not!" I said once in anger. I still regret my response. Maybe I was the one trying to get ready for your death.

Holiness in Our Feelings
2 Samuel 6.12–15; Jeremiah 4.19–22;
Ecclesiastes 3.1–8; Luke 19.41–42
First UMC, Appleton (10/19/86)

[Charlie]

The other day I was walking down the hall here at church and realized that I was singing to myself—Feelings, la, da, da, da, feelings …

"That must have something to do with my sermon," I said out loud to no one in particular. I don't know the words that come in between the la, la, da, da, part, but perhaps that's all right because it is rather hard for some of us to express our feelings—to find words to catch up the inner life.

But even without words our faces often show our feelings. Let's have some fun. I'm going to name some feelings and I want us all to form those feelings on our faces and then look around at each other as we do so. Is that clear? Are you ready? Let's start with anger … despair … love … joy … fear … frustration … pain … curiosity … excitement … loneliness.

Since you can't see your own face, perhaps you'll follow up on this exercise by going home and doing this in a mirror.

[Nancy]

Oh Charlie. You preached on *feelings*! God given and important for a full life with others, you said. When you prompted the congregation to make faces, you must have remembered our dinner at Silvercryst. You know, the restaurant with all those small mirrors lined up over the coatrack in the hallway to the restrooms.

Who started it?

We must have seen our faces in that first mirror when we put on our coats. I still had hair and could see the collar of my new winter coat. You in your suit and tie, of course, smiled and leaned your head toward mine. And suddenly, we were taking turns calling out feelings and hopping from mirror to mirror, laughing and seeing facial expressions that years later would become so familiar to each of us that they didn't need to be named.

For 29 years I had been married to a man who didn't share feelings and whose face remained stolid. I had to determine his moods by a twitch of an eyebrow or his lips scissored into a tight thread.

I miss you. Seeing your face. The crinkles around your blue eyes when you smiled. And we played didn't we? I miss our playing. Our effortless, spontaneous, surprising play.

Jesus' Mission and Ours
Psalm 19; 1 Corinthians 12 (selected); Luke 4.14–21
Little Prairie UMC (1/25/2004)

[Charlie]

One does not stand up and talk in front of people for nearly five decades without there being some embarrassing moments. One such moment for me occurred when I was home from college during Christmas break. Remember that: It's Christmas! It was Sunday morning and the King family, as was their custom, arrived for church about five minutes late. We had missed the call to worship and the opening hymn and caught the end of the responsive reading. Next was the anthem; then the pastor, Paul Krueger, looked right at me and said, "I see that Charles King is home from college. Charles, will you come up and read the Scripture and then offer the morning prayers?"

Well, reading the Bible was no problem, but the pastoral prayers?! I was nervous, and as I searched for some words to say, this sentence came out of my mouth: "O God, on this day when we hear the joyous bells of Easter ..." In a single moment I had moved us through Christmastide, Epiphany and Lent.

– Hometown kid is invited to speak at this house of worship—Charles and Lydia's son.

– Hometown kid is invited to speak at his house of worship—Joseph and Mary's son.

[Nancy]

Great illustration, Charlie. You say "one such moment." There must have been more, but I don't remember you mentioning any. And things didn't go so well for Joseph and Mary's son that day either. He escaped the angry townspeople. *That* time.

Moi? Dozens. Mostly at weddings. Often I didn't know the couple well and sometimes botched up names during the prayer before the banquet. I had no excuse during my own nephew's wedding. All the screwups I did during worship? I learned to laugh at my mistakes right along with the congregation. They were a blessed reminder that I was human.

My mother also let me know my conduct was distasteful. "Thank you for putting up with my daughter," she said to you on more than one occasion. Her oblique swipe hurt. What had I done? She must have felt responsible for my behavior.

Though you didn't say it, I must have embarrassed you numerous times. During gatherings with others, when I peppered conversations with four letter words, only your face clued me in. And then there was the Epiphany party we hosted for your staff. I kept my language pure, but after we ate, I hauled out all those dreadful religious music boxes I'd been given from church members over the years: the snow-globe Jesus hauling his cross to the tune of "The Old Rugged Cross;" Jesus draped over the Gethsemane Rock to "Rock of Ages;" Jesus, standing arms outstretched in swirls of gold-glitter snow to "Amazing Grace." With no thought to others' sensibilities of the sacred, I unboxed each tasteless representation with a snide comment. Though a few folks grinned at my show and tell, most were quiet and the party broke up soon after.

    You and I cleaned up in silence.

    Today is December 23. My second Christmas without you. The only decorations I put up are the skinny fake tree with a string of blue lights, a poinsettia I bought at *Milaeger's*, and an old snow-globe of the holy family that I found after twenty-five years. I had to put new batteries in it so that the light under the Baby Jesus will shine.

War in Heaven and on Earth
Revelation 12 (selected); James 1.12–15
First UMC, Kenosha (5/9/1999)

[Charlie]

    ... So how do we reconcile these points of view—those who believe in the Devil or Satan and those who do not? Or can we? ... Some of you may wish to personify evil—to think of Satan using some of the Biblical imagery that John and others used; others of you may have some theological problems doing that. ... In my opinion the search for the demonic powers leads right to our own human hearts.

    You and I play the role of the devil whenever we resist God, for there is no greater enemy of God than a rebellious creature of God. You and I play the role of the devil when we pull others down to a lower level of moral life through what we have said or done. That's hard for many to take, and I grant that it is more comfortable to place the blame for evil and sin on someone or something outside ourselves. But are we just fooling ourselves and avoiding responsibility in the process?

As someone said on the radio yesterday morning as he was reflecting on the school shootings in Colorado and similar recent events: "There has been lots of *assigning* responsibility for what happened and very little *taking* of responsibility."

[Nancy]

Charlie, if you were still alive we would talk about the latest school shooting, this time in Oxford, Michigan on November 30. Four students dead. Seven injured. The kid responsible isn't talking and today's *New York Times* reports that the parents are going to be charged.

The devil? A definition I like is hinderer—that which prevents us from wholeness. Though you and I agreed on evil residing in our hearts, we didn't agree on how to deal with it. You wanted to suppress it. I wanted to learn to explore it. Cut through the hindering. Embrace the shadow ala Carl Jung.

Yesterday, during a mindfulness meditation at the Blue Christmas service, when the pastor said, "Check your body to see if there is a place you are holding grief," I expected my stomach would do one of its lurches, but immediately my throat began tickling. This rarely happens, but when it does, I keep coughing until I get a lozenge or drink of water. Luckily, I had gum in my purse and managed to unwrap a piece quietly, lift my mask and stick it in my mouth. The sweet syrup quelled my coughing and my anxiety about coming down with Covid, but what was my throat telling me about this cloud of grief I'm lost in? I remembered those years when I couldn't speak at all in a group. Is there something I'm afraid to let escape?

This morning, while making soup, the ginger jar lid jumped out of my hand and rolled under the refrigerator. I swore. And, there it was. Anger. I am pissed all the time. Little things. My purse strap getting caught in the door handle, a new detour on the closest route to my friend's, or pushing the wrong button on the damn remote.

I looked in my quote journal for the Rilke quote—*Our fears are like dragons guarding our most precious treasures*—and found the quote from a February, 2001 *Psychology Today* article:

> Deep in the recesses of our being there are safe sanctuaries, secure hiding places for salvageable dreams. Anger sustains our stubborn refusal to accept others' dire predictions. Anger protects our hopes and dreams.

I don't know why I'm crying. I don't know my own hopes and dreams anymore. I do know I am *angry* at not being allowed to be with you during those last four months of your life.

Covid-19 caused the hindering then. Now Delta. Omicron. We're all being hindered by the Greek alphabet and I don't know where the evil lies or where to assign responsibility.

Pray for the Living and the Dead
Acts 12.1–17
First UMC, Kenosha (5/25/1997)

[Charlie]
This spring we have been talking about the spiritual works of mercy that the church compiled many centuries ago. Today we conclude that list with number seven: "To pray for the living and the dead."

Pray for the living. That I understand; and that I do. But this seventh spiritual work of mercy? ... The context for this act came out of the Roman Catholic Church and its belief that following life here on earth the dead spend time in purgatory. There all who have died suffer until they are purged of their unforgiven venial sins and complete their punishment imposed by God for their mortal sins. The Catholic church teaches that souls in purgatory can be aided by prayers for the dead as well as Masses said for the dead.

Prayers that the dead might be released from purgatory do not make sense to us for there is no justification for purgatory in the Bible.

"But perhaps there is some truth behind the statement (praying for the dead) which should be lifted up," I said to the wall in front of me on Wednesday. And then a picture formed in my mind. Last month I spent three days at a "Church Vision" conference held at First United Methodist Church in Goshen, Indiana. While I was there it occurred to me that I was just about an hour away from Niles, Michigan and the cemetery where my parents were buried. I had not been there for nine years so I skipped one of the workshops and drove to Niles. I stood at my parents' graves and prayed.

As I think now on the time I spent there, I recognize that I uttered prayers of thanksgiving to them for the life and example they set for me. I told them about my wife, Nancy, my children and grandchildren; I heard myself asking them and/or God for direction and guidance as I grow older. I also found myself doing some quick mathematical calculations as I subtracted the dates of their birth and deaths to get their ages at the time of their deaths and then compare them with my current age.

You know, praying for the dead—or in the presence of the dead—makes us confront the mystery of life and death.

[Nancy]
Charlie. What can I say? You have been dead 15 months. Pray for you? What would *that* look like? A few weeks after your death, the ineffective hospice counselor suggested I write letters to you and see what your answers would be. I poured out my heart into a soft-covered journal for months and … nothing … nothing from you. Wasn't I praying?

When she called again and I told her you weren't responding, she said something like "Oh." She quit calling.

Sweetheart. You told me about visiting your parents' graves. You didn't tell me what you prayed. In fact, we rarely discussed our prayers. You used words. I meditated. A few times we tried a ritual at breakfast. After eating, we took turns reading a short selection from a book. Except for Frederick Buechner's *Wishful Thinking: A Theological ABC*, our commitments only lasted a few days. We seemed to respond to different types of devotional options as well as praying.

When I was young, I thought prayer was a cry from the heart to some old man in the sky.

While I was leading churches, I used Jack Biersdorf's definition: *Prayer is living as if the God of Love were the fundamental reality in the Universe and in your life.* Now? I still have two fat file folders titled prayer and prayer exercises.

None of the hundreds of pages mentions praying for the dead.

When a church member requested prayer, I always asked "What are *you* praying for?"

But you? I don't know what prayers you might want or need?

Maybe these responses to your sermons are my prayers for you. Maybe these cries from my heart are what you need.

Peace and Persecution
Matthew 5.9–10
Wauwatosa Avenue UMC (3/20/2016)

[Charlie]
Now I usually read the first draft of my sermons to Nancy and she writes a few comments as I read—things I wrote that were unclear, words to cut out, and possible additions to the sermons. But last Sunday afternoon as I read what I had written so far, she was writing notes throughout today's entire sermon. "Give personal examples," she said, after I finished reading. "What actions have you taken on behalf of justice and then been persecuted for it?"

After a couple of minutes of silence, I said to Nancy ... "I could tell about the time in First Church Appleton when, during the second service a man came in, walked to the front of the church, carrying a bucket filled with blood, and threw that blood all over the front pews, our new rug, and communion railing. He was opposed to our church's public position regarding abortion."

Well, I lay awake in bed last Sunday night for the next two hours, unable to sleep, thinking of other examples that illustrated the beatitudes of Peace and Persecution.

[Nancy]
Oh, Charlie, I remember you telling me about that shocking disruption. I was in my last term at seminary and didn't

witness the mess. How horrible this event must have been for you. The news hit the next day's Appleton *Post Crescent*. Several times over the years, you shared it with friends and colleagues, but here you are telling it to a church full of people.

Your memory of this upsetting interruption prompted my search for the sermon you preached the following Sunday, February 17, 1985. Your text then was from the book of James: "What good is it for someone to say 'I have faith' if actions do not prove it." I was surprised that you didn't mention the bloody scene until the end of your sermon as a segue to lead the congregation in a prayer to ritually cleanse the sanctuary space. Rather, your illustrations were anecdotes from people who demonstrated their Christian faith by the actions they took on behalf of justice: An archbishop, the Apostle Paul, the current chair of the Consumer Product Safety Commission.

You even quoted some doggerel:

Faith is not valid—in fact it's rather pallid;
Your words are hard to swallow, unless actions follow.

Still curious about the details of that thirty-five-year-old event, I contacted the research librarian at the Racine Public Library and a day later she emailed me a copy of the February 11, 1985 Appleton *Post-Crescent* article. Details of the disturbing action were included, as well as several church members' quick response to restrain the man until police arrived and arrested him.

Though the sermon preached after the stunning disruption and the preceding sermon have differing Biblical texts they have a similar theme: Faith must lead to actions and those actions from faith may result in persecution.

But as you prepared either of these sermons did you consider that the anti-abortion protestor might have been acting out of *his* faith?

Wondering about what happened to him, I googled his name and discovered an obituary. Though the dates and location seemed to fit, I wasn't sure that I had the right man until I read, "In 1984, Jerry made 'the best decision' of his life, to accept Jesus as his personal Savior, leaving a Godly legacy for his family."

At age 36, this man gave his life to Jesus. Less than a year later, he splashed his faith all over the First United Methodist Church sanctuary. Was he acting out of his faith understanding?

Oh Charlie. You began slipping into dementia during the second year of Trump. You've missed the attack on the Capitol, the deadly fallout from the pandemic, and the recalcitrant anger that divides our country. This morning's *New York Times* reported the fire that destroyed a Planned Parenthood health clinic in Knoxville, Tennessee on 12/31/21 was caused by arson.

What would you be preaching now?

Celebrate the Temporary
Luke 12.23-31; Philippians 4.10–13
First UMC, Kenosha (7/1/1990)

[Charlie]

This spring some of us were anxiously awaiting the next television episode of "Twin Peaks" to learn who killed Laura Palmer. On one show FBI Agent Dale Cooper was sitting in the Twin Peaks restaurant and said to his companion: "Every day, once a day, give yourself a present. Don't plan it, don't wait for it. Just let it happen …"

"Give yourself a present." That's what I want to talk about today. "Celebrate the Temporary," is another way to express that same thought. In fact, that is the title of a book by

Clyde Reid. When I read that book about fifteen years ago it was important to me and definitely influenced my outlook on life. You see, nearly everything around us seems to conspire to keep us from living in the present—in the now...

... an important step if we are to celebrate the temporary is to learn to let go ... an important aspect of letting go is what is called "letting your child out to play." Our adult roles call for us to be serious and straight for so much of the time that we often forget to enjoy life. Yet Jesus calls us to be as little children. Experience childness occasionally: blow bubbles, skip down the sidewalk instead of walking, read a Dr. Seuss book out loud to yourself, walk through a puddle, skip rocks across the water, throw a snowball, have a fight with water pistols, put a red nose on ...

... And there's this advice from Charlie King: Give yourself a present. Spend $1.35 for a single deluxe chocolate chip cookie and spend fifteen minutes slowly sharing it with someone you love ...

[Nancy]

One picky thing. You called yourself "Charlie King." Of course, we'd only been married a couple months and I suppose you were still getting used to your new surname, the one we shared, Bauer-King.

Other than that, I'm glad I found this sermon. The Clyde Reid book obviously influenced you because you've mentioned it before. Though your discussion includes paying attention to the past and future as well as the necessity and danger of letting go, this time your examples are fresh and personal. I cried and laughed as I read this because I'm definitely in it.

Oh, you don't name me, but I'm the one who brought the bubbles, bought the cookie, and gave you the clown nose.

And, while I was doing my Field Ed requirement, I was the one who clomped in my blue clogs down the long hallway toward the church offices on my way home from seminary for the weekend. "Can anyone come out and play?" I hollered.

You came out of your office, a big grin on your face. We walked out the back door of the church, through the bank parking lot and across College Avenue to the Casbah for a cup of coffee. I treated. You used cream. I had only known you about a year and didn't like you very much then. You were too effusive. Too happy. And, too black and white.

But you were the only one who came out to play with me.

It's ironic that at the end of your life the fog of dementia destined you to live completely in the temporary. You stood at the window looking out at the lake. Counted geese flying by. Watched the squirrel try to get into the bird feeder.

We didn't play.

Faithfulness, Faith, and Freedom
Galatians 1.1–12; 6.17a
First UMC, Kenosha (6/18/95)

[Charlie]
More times than I can remember I have people coming to me raving and praising something they heard on television or witnessed at someone else's worship service, or read in some book or other. And my response has usually been a polite inquiry. "Oh, tell me about that. What was it that appealed to you? How will that be helpful to you?" And so on.

Occasionally, I will make some mild criticism or quote some Scripture passage or I'll say that is not my understanding of the Christian faith, but inside I'm often thinking of what Paul put in print. The heresies of ancient times are still with us but in our politically correct, tolerant world we sometimes lack the courage of Paul who let it be known that it is fatal to go back on the truth.

[Nancy]

Heresy. A great word. Truth. Another great word. I've been called weird and iconoclastic, but not a heretic.

Yet.

I did have to deal with George Franklin who was convinced he knew the truth. He stopped in the office regularly bringing me tapes, newspaper articles and strong opinions. He wanted me to scold people from the pulpit. People *other* than him, of course. After six years of waiting for me to preach hellfire and brimstone, George grew angry and petitioned the UMC to get rid of all women pastors.

Thankfully, Facebook hadn't been invented yet.

Charlie, maybe it was easier for you to react calmly to theological misunderstandings because you didn't have to withstand attacks on your gender.

Jesus Through the Eyes of the Crowd
Luke 9.18–20; John 15.12–17
First UMC, Appleton (3/27/1988)

[Charlie]
Let's begin this morning by thinking of some occasions when we have been a part of a crowd of people ... and now let's see if you can name the emotions that arose within you as you were in those crowds ...

I did most of my reflecting this Thursday afternoon. Being a part of crowds at sports events came immediately to my mind; the accompanying emotions were excitement and disappointment depending on how my teams were doing. I also remembered crowds in La Paz, Bolivia protesting government actions—curious Charlie King was often in the midst of them; and once soldiers shot at the crowd to scatter us; we scattered and the emotion I felt was fear. And I thought of times I've felt loneliness even while many people were around.

Yes. The emotions we feel are dependent upon the circumstances, the settings, the nature of the crowds.

[Nancy]
You preached this on Palm Sunday in 1988. Crowds in Jerusalem. Jesus on the donkey. Hosanna. Hosanna. Save us. Save us.

Last Saturday my southeastern Wisconsin kin met at *Fork in the Road* for lunch to celebrate Thanksgiving. There were seven of us at the table. A small crowd. Lots of laughing. I was happy. Contented. We remembered childhood Thanksgivings. I mentioned the gatherings at Great Aunt Nelle's where I felt warm and safe in the middle of a crowd of at least 20.

During our lunch on Saturday, your name was mentioned once. "I cry," I said. "I do too," my sister said. We're both widows. I hate the word.

Then I got in the car for the 55-minute drive home. As I was driving out of the restaurant's parking lot, the comfort and light of the past two hours began dissipating like smoke from an extinguished candle. By the time I accelerated up the ramp to merge into I-43 traffic I was sinking into the being alone chasm again.

Most of the time I don't mind being alone, but, Charlie, when your absence fills me with numbing sorrow, I hear the cry of that ancient crowd. Save me. Save me.

Life Has Meaning
Luke 18.18–27
First UMC, Kenosha (6/13/99)

[Charlie]
Three years ago this month, Nancy and I moved into our own home. When asked, I've prefaced my comments about the joys, costs, and problems associated with home ownership by telling people, "It's the first time in 37 years that I haven't lived in a house owned by the church." But I'm learning that ownership of anything—a great pearl, a home, whatever—can lead to possessiveness and idolatry, and then danger!

[Nancy]
Ah. You preached on the "pearl of great price," the guy who sees a pearl and sells everything he has in order to buy it. A few weeks ago, I facilitated a class discussion on this story from

the Gospel of Luke, a story that prompts reflection upon ultimate value. One question the story poses is "Would you be willing to give away *everything* you have in order to obtain *some one thing*? What would it be?

The folks in the class had difficulty answering the question. Me, too.

Five days ago, December 10, tornados cut a devastating swath through the Midwest. So far 88 people are dead and 100 still unaccounted for. The media blared stories of loss. One man, who while rummaging through the wreckage of his home, found a purple heart still in its frame, completely undamaged. The man choked up while relating the importance of finding this one remnant. Most individuals interviewed were simply grateful to be alive.

Is there one thing that I would give everything to obtain?

Yes. To relive the morning of September 10, 2020. To arrive at Burr Oak Manor in time. To be given more than fifteen minutes with your dead body to say goodbye. To say how much I love you. To say how grateful I am for sharing your life with me. To thank you for all the gifts you gave.

The Shortness of Life
1 Corinthians 15.12–22
First UMC, Kenosha (1/9/2000)

[Charlie]
One Easter Sunday morning about thirty-five years ago, I stood before my congregation in the La Paz Community Church and began my sermon by telling the people that two of them sitting there that morning probably would die within the next

year. At least the statistical averages so indicated this probability. I found out a few months later that three persons who heard me make that statement vowed never to come back to that church again. It seems that these folks were so deeply disturbed by this reminder of the shortness of life that they then shut their ears to the Easter message—the message that death has been overcome! It is simply fact that each of us needs to prepare for death—our own, as well as those we love.

Life is short! But every day is a new day of grace, a new day to forgive and to ask forgiveness, a new day to grow and experience joy. A new day to celebrate the temporary.

[Nancy]
Charlie, you told this story several times over the years. Different churches, of course, but here it is again, the same story, thirty-five years later. You obviously took those departures personally and learned early in your ministry how your words could affect folks' lives. I wonder if this story affected you, too. You were 28 when you preached it the first time. Did you consider that during the next year you might be one of the two to die?

Somewhere during those ensuing years, you began to see the value of enjoying the moments given. In this sermon you credited the phrase "celebrate the temporary" to the title of a book you read in 1975 by Clyde Reid. You shared how you began to pay attention to the time given to you, but when I met you, almost ten years after you read Reid's book, you were still working 70+ hour weeks.

"Don't you take a day off?" I asked during the year you were my Field Ed supervisor.

"Yes," you answered. "I take Tuesdays off."

"But *today* is Tuesday."

"I know. But I don't have a tie on. I don't wear ties on Tuesdays."

After we married, I talked you into taking Fridays off. Wedding rehearsals and funerals often interrupted. How many times had we planned a movie, a drive to see my mother, or catch Metra to Chicago, and a funeral director called to inform one of us of a member's death?

Each of those deaths reminded us of our own mortality, that we only had the day—and the moment—we were given.

Charlie, in this sermon, you refer to a quote from the wife of Medgar Evers, shortly after he was shot:

> *In a funny way, the constant threat of death made life richer and more meaningful—it made us more aware of each other and it brought us closer together. When he left in the morning, I never knew if I would see him again. We never parted in anger, because we couldn't afford to.*

Then in your sermon you add, "There is an old saying about not going to sleep angry with your spouse; have things resolved before sleep. I don't want to dismiss that wise saying, but much more often I remember the words of Medgar Evers' wife and try not to leave the house in the *morning* with issues unresolved between Nancy and me. We might not see each other again."

Sweetheart. The last time I saw you alive were those few seconds you were being carried from the ambulance into Burr Oak. Because of Covid, I was kept about fifteen feet away. All I could do was holler, "Charlie, I love you!"

I trust you heard me.

Sing of Hope and Healing
Isaiah 35.1–18; James 5.7–10; Matthew 11.2–11
Emanuel UMC, Milwaukee (12/12/2004)

[Charlie]

It was Christmas Eve in Appleton about twenty years ago. I was responsible for leading the worship at the late candlelight service. It was a service of music, Scripture readings, poetry, and stories. One of the stories I read was by South African Bishop Desmond Tutu. The story ended with a request by the bishop that as Christians light candles on Christmas Eve in our churches, we would remember the oppression and violence and poverty and racism in his country and pray for the people of South Africa.

Well, as I stood at the church door at the end of the service wishing people a "Holy Christmas," Bill, one of the chronic complainers of the church, came up with an even more pronounced scowl on his face than usual.

"Well, you sure ruined my Christmas with that service," he said.

"What do you mean?" I asked.

"That stuff about South Africa and racism doesn't belong in a Christmas service!"

I don't remember how I responded, but I probably was very defensive and not very loving.

Where did Bill think Jesus was born? Why did he think Jesus was born anyway? What was he thinking about when we sang, "Hail to the Lord's Anointed" and its words, "He comes to those who suffer wrong; to help the poor and needy, and bid the weak be strong; to give them songs for sighing, their darkness turned to light …"

[Nancy]

Your interaction with Bill reminds me of that old advice to preachers: "Your job is to comfort the afflicted and afflict the comfortable." Maybe Bill wanted comfort and your words afflicted him. Who knows?

To respond to Bill's criticism, you quote verse two of "Hail to the Lord's Anointed." I chose that hymn once every Advent, the liturgical season that represents the centuries our faith ancestors waited and waited and waited—hoping for light. Advent is my favorite season of the church year because it's dark. I like dark. I like looking, silently, waiting to see what "light" will show up.

Folks I served didn't get into Advent. Christmas was on their mind. They were busy with shopping and decorating and baking. They wanted to get right to the sweet baby Jesus songs. But I needed songs for sighing, songs for remembering the dark times I'd experienced and how I'd survived.

Especially this year, I need songs for sighing. You aren't here and another variant of Covid-19 is messing up folks' plans. For the first time ever, on Christmas Day I'll be alone.

Faithfulness, Faith, and Freedom
Galatians 1.1–12; 6.17a
First UMC, Kenosha   (6/18/95)

[Charlie]

I am so grateful that my first years after seminary graduation were spent in Bolivia. There I witnessed people putting llama fetus' under the foundations of the houses they built so as to appease the gods; I saw them pour out wine on the ground as a sacrifice to Mother Earth before they began to plant their crops; I saw them kneel at shrines built at mountain passes where they prayed for God's protection as they made their journey; I saw the bonfires on the Day of St. John—the coldest day of the year—set to encourage the warmth of the sun to return to the southern hemisphere. Those attempts to appease the gods or manipulate fate by making sacrifices were rather obvious and blatant; but there are *many* ways in which we are controlled by superstitions and gods of our own making and rules and laws which we think will bring us good fortune, or luck, or God's blessing, or at least keep us and our family out of trouble.

But the message of Paul to the Galatians and to the Bolivians, and to us right now, is a message of freedom from all those things that enslave us—a message of God's love given to us even though we haven't followed all the rules and rituals ...

[Nancy]

Today is Christmas and for the first time in my life, I'm alone. The rest of the world—well, *some* of the rest of the world—is celebrating the birth of Jesus. Me? I put red peppers and left-over cooked broccoli in my breakfast omelet to give the eggs, onions, and mushrooms Christmas colors. I spent the rest of the day reading the *New York Times*, the preface to *The 1619 Project*, and writing thank yous for gifts I received.

Now I'm here with you and your words of faith, faithfulness, and freedom. What can I say?

Sue called on Thursday. "I have something to ask you," the pastor said. "I might cry..."

"Okay ..." I answered. *What happened? What does she want?*

I wait.

"I'm preaching the Simeon and Anna story on Sunday. I'd like to wear Charlie's Bolivian stole. You know, that fantastic one you draped over the worship table the morning we did the ritual for him. Remember? The same morning I baptized Everett."

How could I forget that Sunday? Because of Covid-19, the service was held outside on the church lawn, a month after you died and six weeks after Everett's birth. Death and new life in the congregation celebrated during the same worship service.

"When I pictured Simeon," Sue continued, her words faltering, "I pictured an old man with gnarled hands picking up the baby Jesus. Then I thought of Charlie. I don't know if Charlie's hands were gnarled…"

I see your hands. Soft. Smooth. Not one arthritic knob pushing your joints askew.

"…and I remembered Charlie's stole. If it's okay with you I'd like to wear that stole on Sunday."

I see your stole, the colorful scenes of Bolivian life hand-embroidered by women in your church and given to you when you left your ministry there.

"Of course, it's okay," I told Sue and reached for Kleenex. "But that stole is in Boston now. Charlie's son has it along with other articles to remember his dad. However, I do have a stole that Charlie used for baptisms. If you want that one, I can drop it off in the office."

I took the stole in yesterday afternoon. On Sunday, I'll sit in the back pew next to the box of Kleenex.

Good Gossip and Bad
James 3.1–12; 4.11–12
First UMC, Appleton (5/8/88)

[Charlie]
Last week two things happened which struck me as interesting because of their stark contrast: One was our annual Council on Ministries Planning Retreat. Last Sunday evening there was a lot of excitement and optimism as nearly two dozen people began a process of thinking through plans and programs for one, two, three, four, and five years from now. "First in the Nineties" we called it.

And then there was a report I received about a member who has become super-critical and was gossiping about this church and its pastors and its mission and its direction. "This church is dead," he said.

That was disturbing to hear, of course. At first it hurt deeply, not only because his bad gossip could actually contribute to the death of a church, but also because it does cause a small death in me. I worked it through. After a time, I came to the realization that the kind of a church this person really wants is a dead church in the nineties. At least that's what will happen if he has his way.

You see: live churches constantly change their methods. Dead churches don't have to. Live churches have noisy kids. Dead churches are quiet. Live churches exceed their income. Dead churches take in more than they can spend. Live churches plan for the future. Dead churches worship their past. Live churches grow so fast you forget people's names. Dead churches know everyone's name. Live churches support missions heavily. Dead churches keep it all at home. Live churches are filled with tithers. Dead churches are filled with tippers. Live churches dream great dreams. Dead churches relive nightmares. Live churches have the fresh wind of love. Dead churches are stale with bickering. Live churches don't have *can't* in their vocabulary. Dead churches have nothing but. Live churches have evocative, pertinent preaching. Dead churches have insipid, irrelevant preaching. Live churches evangelize. Dead churches fossilize.

[Nancy]

Whoa. Charlie, your paragraph contrasting live and dead churches reads like a litany. Poetic. While you claimed you were not a poet, we wrote each other poems during those first exciting falling-in-love months. I've lost all your poems but one: Swings.

Do you remember writing it?

> *When I was a boy ...*
> *When I was a parent of young children ...*
> *When I was in love ...*

You described your rope swing, your grandparent's swing, the playground swing with your kids, and the Lutz Park swing. I printed your words in calligraphy around a pencil sketch of our swing and put it into an old frame. The frame is falling apart. The wire and nails are rusty, but your words of love for me are vibrant.

And so were all the churches you served.

The Characteristics of Christians
Romans 12.1–2, 9–11, 21
First UMC, Kenosha (7/9/89)

[Charlie]
    ... I remember early in my life that when people would challenge me with some question like, "Are you really a Christian?" my response was to say rather timidly, "Well, I'm *trying* to be." But I stopped doing that long ago. Now I affirm as strongly as I can, "Yes, I am!" I want it understood that the basic commitment for the direction of my life is down the path that Jesus walked. I *know* that God loves me, forgives me, and accepts me.

[Nancy]
    Yes. Your actions affirmed you knew you were loved, forgiven and accepted. All your life you knew. I was 30 before I felt that it was okay for me to be on the earth. Just okay. To know I was loved? That came from being with you over the years. Learning to trust you, trusting myself.
    I don't know what well of mystery you drew your living water from, but I'm forever grateful you shared it with me. At least enough to experience moments of refreshing joy.
    Charlie, do you remember hearing Maya Angelou when we were in D.C.?
    "When somebody tells me they are Christian," she said, "I respond, 'Already?'"
    Me? I was baptized so I guess Christian is one of my labels regarding organized religion, but what about faith? What do I have *faith* in? More to the point, in *Whom* do I have faith?

Blind Samson
Judges 13–16 (portions)
First UMC, Kenosha (9/23/1990)

[Charlie]
    Throughout September we pastors are sharing with you some of the Bible stories we remember from our days in Sunday School. For me this week the choice narrowed down between David and Goliath or Samson. Finally, and I'm not sure why, I chose Samson—perhaps because in reading the stories about him I discovered a lot I had forgotten or perhaps never had been taught in Sunday School. Come to think of it, my teachers at Mt. Washington Methodist Church never did explain clearly what Samson was doing in Delilah's bedroom.

[Nancy]
    Oh Charlie. You preached about Samson a few years later. You don't go any further into Delilah's bedroom in either sermon. Why not? You immediately launch into Philistine history and the story of Samson. Too bad. Folks who may have been on the edge of their pew alert for an x-rated story, probably slid back. Disappointed.
    Someone once said that for 2,000 years the Christian church has avoided dealing with sex and anger. And, here's horny Samson, who in a fit of pique, kills a thousand Philistines with the jawbone of an ass. What an opportunity to deal with both *sex and anger* in one twenty-minute shot. Instead, you go for the violence and the ongoing animosity between Philistia and Israel.
    You also remind folks that for centuries the Hebrews faced one enemy after another and add they would have enjoyed telling the tales of this Paul Bunyan-type hero. At least you

acknowledge Samson's negative behavior as something not to emulate.

    Charlie, did you ever figure out why you chose the story of Samson instead of David? We'd been married only four months when you preached this sermon. What was happening in *our* bedroom was of biblical proportions. And, definitely private.

Love is Not Rude or Selfish
1 Corinthians 13.5
Oconomowoc UMC (3/16/1980)

[Charlie]
    "Love is not rude." I looked up the meaning of the word "rude" in my dictionary last week. It means: discourteous; impolite; without culture, learning, or refinement; uncouth. That scared me. How can I preach for twenty minutes about not being discourteous? I'm not Emily Post or Miss Manners. A sermon is not supposed to be a lecture in etiquette. But I read on in Paul's letter to Corinth: "Love does not insist on its own way," says the Revised Standard Version. "Love does not pursue selfish advantage," says the Phillips translation. And, with that some ideas began to come to mind.

    … As I thought about this subject last week, I began to picture times when we are rude; and lest we think that rudeness has only to do with not opening a car door for someone, or not knowing the proper way to make introductions, I'd like to share with you my expanded understanding of rudeness …

[Nancy]

Ah. You preached this back when twenty-minute sermons were expected. You preached this sermon years before we met, years before I had the occasion to see how you treated waitresses. Eventually, after I told you the waitress probably was a mother working on a couple dollars an hour wage and deserved not to be hollered at, but deserved a 20 percent tip, (*at least*), you quit your restaurant rudeness.

Though you spend a couple of paragraphs on rudeness—not listening to or attempting to understand others—you spent most of your sermon discussing the importance of good communication.

Especially in marriage.

While you were preaching this sermon, I had just celebrated my 40th birthday and the only thing I remember from that momentous day is the card from my mother. The front of the card has the Norman Rockwell painting of a couple sitting at a breakfast table. The husband, dressed in a suit, is hidden behind an open newspaper he is reading. The wife, coffee cup in hand, is staring off in the distance. Written above the couple is the greeting: *They say life begins at forty…* and inside the card? … *begins to WHAT?*

Did my mother know the Rockwell picture was a perfect portrayal of the communication in my marriage then? None. Communication almost non-existent.

At forty, although my life's *beginnings* were hesitant, hashed over with counselors, and helped with anti-depressants, I was beginning to heed my own longings. At 41, my former spouse and I moved into a passive solar home I designed. At 42, I entered seminary.

Love and Marriage
Exodus 20.14
Oconomowoc UMC (9/14/1980)

[Charlie]

While working on this sermon concerning adultery, the seventh commandment, I rephrased the command for the children's sermon. "You shall have a good marriage." I wasn't just trying to avoid talking to second and third graders about adultery; I really believe that if the seventh commandment is to be kept, we must understand the nature of marriage itself.

…This summer I spent spare moments going through five years back issues of *Reader's Digest* magazines—clipping some things, reading and re-reading a few articles. Doing that makes one quite aware of the formula writing that is done for that periodical. There are themes repeated in issue after issue. Nearly every issue had some sort of article about love and making your marriage better in a few easy steps. It's not my intention to present that sort of thing today, but I do want to share with you my personal feelings about what has made our own marriage a good marriage.

It's not my normal way to get quite this personal in sermons and it's really putting your own marriage in the spotlight, but these words today are uttered from experience—in our home and from seeing what has not worked in couples who have come to share their problems with me.

[Nancy]

Charlie. I should have thrown this sermon out unread. You described *eleven* factors that contributed to your twenty-year happy marriage to your former spouse. Picturing you trusting, talking, having fun with her stirred up jealousy and bile.

Yet, eight years later, almost to the day, your divorce was final.

What happened? Something must have been missing in your *good* marriage.

We talked about it, of course. We did a *lot* of talking. Lots of communication. Something that didn't happen with my former spouse.

Because we talked things through, I really thought when we got married, we wouldn't have any conflict. How wrong! There was conflict. Nothing major, but little things loomed. We argued over the amount of money to spend on gifts for our children and grandchildren, when to call the church trustees about the broken dishwasher, and your organizing. Your *constant* organizing. Reorganizing. Files in the basement, books on the shelves, tools in the garage. There was the day I came back from my walk and discovered you had dumped my $13.50 a pound Sumatran coffee in with the cheap Aldi. Pat and Carl next door probably heard my shrieking.

But I notice in this series on The Ten Commandments you don't really discuss adultery. Rather you say that to keep the seventh commandment, we need to understand the nature of marriage. After a few more innocuous comments you launch into your self-righteous list.

Shortly after I met you, a colleague referred to you as a "straight arrow." Maybe in those days you were.

I Believe
Mark 9.14–27
First UMC, Kenosha (9/12/99)

[Charlie]

We begin today a series of sermons that will look at what Christians believe today—in other words: What is this reality, that mystery which is beyond us, which we name and to which we give our allegiance?

At one time or other we all ask questions such as these: Who am I and why am I here? Are we alone in the universe? What is God like? What am I searching for? What happens when I die? The conclusions we eventually work out come as statements about our beliefs.

... Now a sermon about belief that doesn't acknowledge skepticism and doubt isn't complete in my opinion. That's why I really appreciate having the incident recorded in the New Testament that took place between Jesus and the man who had a sick son. "If you are able to do anything...help us!" the man cried. "All things can be done for the one who believes," said Jesus. And the father cried out at once, "I believe; help my unbelief!"

Or there is this translation from the Good News which I like: "I do have faith, but not enough. Help me have more!" There is the ambiguity boldly set before us—belief and unbelief—this mixture of the two with which we *all* live.

[Nancy]

Was it coincidence this sermon appeared at the top of the stack this morning? You raised the issue of ambiguity—belief and unbelief. A week ago, I received Pauline Boss' book *The Myth of Closure: Ambiguous Loss in Time of Pandemic and Change*. Because I worry sometimes about how much I am crying, I turned immediately to Chapter 8: "If Not Closure, What's Normal Grief." Two paragraphs evoked more tears:

> *I want to be frank with you: you can be knocked down and eventually get up again to have a good life, but you'll never be completely over the loss of someone you have loved.*
>
> *There is no closure, nor is there a need for it. Instead, we remember them and learn to live with the ambiguity of absence and presence. You know they're gone, but you keep them present in your heart and mind—even as you move forward with your life. They become part of your psychological family.*

Charlie. When I read this there were more than tears. I sobbed. I don't know if it's normal. I don't care. At least the ambiguity of loss is named. Your death has called my beliefs into question. I have no idea where you are or even *if* you are.

In referring to faith, you said, "We yearn for certainty." You lightened up the somber reflection with a Woody Allen quote. *If God would only speak to me—just once. If God would only cough. If I could just see a miracle. If I could see a burning bush or the seas part. Or my Uncle Abe pick up the check.*

Did people laugh? I hope so.

Boss, whose husband died during the pandemic, says "resilience is our best hope in the face of ambiguous loss." She offers six guidelines for resilience.

She doesn't include humor. One of my favorite survival techniques.

Born of the Spirit
John 3.1–8; Romans 8.9–11; Galatians 5.22–23a
First UMC, Kenosha (1/15/1995)

[Charlie]

I'd like for you to learn a Hebrew word today, or remind you of a word you've heard before. It's *ruach*. This single word has three meanings in English. It means "breath" –as in the breath of life. It also means the desert wind in the Middle East, which blows so violently and destructively at times. And third, it means the Spirit of God, the power that sweeps across the ages, bursts into history, and takes possession of the lives of people.

The reference to the desert wind reminded me of my experience in Saudi Arabia in a windstorm—where plows are used to clear the roads of sand much as we use our machinery to clear them of snow drifts. And I thought of other experiences with wind. I've got some good stories; most of us probably do. Suppose we got into groups of two or three right here today and told each other some of our experiences with wind! I imagine the room would fill with conversation. Then suppose I changed the rules and asked each person to talk about his and her experiences with the Spirit of God. Would the same level of conversational noise be apparent? Or would there be silence? Embarrassment? Anxiety?

[Nancy]

Good sermon, Charlie. But I don't like your initial definition of Spirit of God. Bursting into history and taking possession of people's lives? I think the whole cosmos is Spirit. Spirit already within and around us, something we're *in*. Not something that bursts in and takes possession of us. And, frankly, I have more stories about my experiences with Spirit than I do with wind. My only wind story is the blustery day we were walking around the square in some little Wisconsin town and the fickle breath of some god or other lifted the wig off my head and sent it tumbling down the sidewalk like some hairy tumbleweed. From then on, any breeze threatened mortifying embarrassment.

Sometime during Bardo—those forty days after your death—I quit wearing the wig. I no longer care about the wind. *Ruach* playing with my sparse hair is freeing.

Your reference to Saudi Arabia? A gold ring you bought there reminded you of your two months of ministry in that country of sand, oil, and Spirit. Every day since the intake worker at Bolingbrook's geriatric psych hospital slipped it off your finger and gave it to me, I've worn the reminder of you.

Simon of Cyrene
Mark 15.16–21
Oconomowoc UMC (3/25/81)

[Charlie]
    Whenever I talk about cross-bearing, I'm afraid that we have trouble with this because people don't go around our community carrying wooden cross pieces; and we have seen so many pictures of Jesus and the cross, that I for one, get that Biblical scene in my mind's eye immediately. Let me see, then, if I can replace that with another image of bearing the cross and the help that it brings to others...

[Nancy]
    Charlie, I took this paragraph from page five of your sermon about Simon of Cyrene, the guy that the Romans picked out of the crowd to help Jesus carry his cross. You get the Biblical

image of Jesus in your mind's eye. I get the picture of the man in Oconto who actually dragged a cross over his shoulder every year in the Copper Culture parade.

The year was 1985. I had been newly appointed to Abrams and Oconto United Methodist Churches. I learned from my parishioners about the ancient people who once occupied the land, left copper artifacts, and were celebrated every summer with Copper Culture Days. And—oh yes—I was expected to ride on their float in the parade.

They also told me about the man who for several years had hauled his cross along the whole route.

"Don't worry about him," the wife of the lay leader said. "He's weird, but harmless."

I got my first glimpse of him during the parade from my spot perched on an old church pew on the bed of a farm wagon.

My second view of him was through the window of my church office. Though he didn't have his cross, he had another man with him. They both saw me. I was alone. The doors to the church were unlocked. What did they want? I took a deep breath, stepped out of my office and met them at the front door.

"How can I help you?" I asked the guy who played suffering Jesus.

"We just wanted to see what a lady pastor looked like," he said and grinned.

They must have seen my raised eyebrows and set lips because they turned and walked away before I could respond. What did they expect? Horns? Only a few months into my job, I had already dealt with a woman who left the church because I couldn't claim I'd been "slain in the spirit." Others transferred their membership to the Gospel Chapel down the street because they refused to take communion from a woman.

Bearing the cross? I've been ostracized, criticized, and rejected, but never felt like I was bearing anything like a cross.

Anyway, I think the cross-bearing bottom line is to be willing to suffer with. Charlie, you and I both suffered the last few months of your life, but you did a better job than I did, my love. Though you didn't understand my sharp answers, slamming the doors, and sobbing in the shower, you leaned against the wall in the hallway and waited for me to dry off.

"Can you ever forgive me?" you asked, walking toward me with your arms out.

"You didn't do anything to forgive," I answered, so ashamed of my behavior. Why didn't I let you hug me? Or allow myself to hug you?

Fear and Faith
1 John 4.16–19; Psalm 27.1–3; Psalm 46.1–3
First UMC, Kenosha (1/12/1992)

[Charlie]

… What are you afraid of? What do you fear? I'm going to stop talking for a few seconds and let you get a start on making a mental list of your fears …

… I made out my own list on Tuesday. Here's what I wrote down: anger and disapproval of my spouse; the loss of my children's love; that I'll become incompetent as a pastor; that I'll become incapacitated through a stroke or accident; torture (the origin of that last fear comes either from spy novels I've read or from the knowledge of torture which goes on in countries I've lived in and visited—like Bolivia, Argentina, and Chile.)

And with permission I share my wife's list of fears when I asked her: death; pain and dying; abandonment; love; the unknown; rejection; and centipedes.

[Nancy]

Oh … those old lists. You didn't put death on your list and I was surprised *love* showed up on mine. (I laughed when I read centipedes.) But Charlie, neither of us named dementia. As your memory faded, our fears multiplied.

I was in the kitchen the day you burst in the back door, a map of Racine in your right hand. "I couldn't find the emission place," you cried. "I couldn't even find Douglas Avenue."

Instead of allaying your fears, I went to the computer, found the address, and drove us to have the Honda checked.

We were both afraid.

Then Covid-19 hit. My fear grew as the days turned into months. I signed papers, drove to doctor appointments, paid bills, saw a lawyer. And, agonized during those last four long months of your life while we were kept apart.

Today is January 21, 2022. My list has changed. Love? My fear, of course, came from experiencing abuse from adults who said they loved me. Because of your presence in my life, I'm learning to trust love. I think of the William James quote: *We're put on earth a little space to learn to bear the beams of love*. Though I'm no longer as afraid of love as I once was, I have a reverent respect for the searing vulnerability that may be required to experience its depths.

Except for centipedes, I'm not as fearful of the other items I listed thirty years ago and I believe the scripture reference from 1 John 4 is the reason: *Perfect love casts out fear*. Our love for each other was certainly not perfect, but it carried us through the tough times.

Your sermon contained a list of ways to deal with fears: name them; live in the moment; share them with others; faith ... you explicated each of these ways, all of your ideas described well, but you missed laughter. Here's what helps me when the sight of a centipede turns my body into jelly:

>What goes 99 thump? 99 thump?
>A centipede with a wooden leg.

Invitation to Join the Barnabas Club
Acts 4.32a, 36–37; 9.26–28; 11.19–26
Wauwatosa Avenue UMC (10/30/2011)

[Charlie]

... The New Testament tells us a great deal about Barnabas, but the information is scattered throughout the Book of Acts and in three of Paul's letters. ... Today let's look at this Christian leader—not out of curiosity—but because I think we can find here guidance for what it means to respond to the call of Jesus and live a full Christian life. You see, Barnabas was a person who took gifts not much different from those of the average person like you and me and made a great impact. And he did it simply by letting God use him whenever the chance came for him to help somebody else; and in helping others it became clear that he was indeed "a good man, full of the Holy Spirit and faith."

... Barnabas: he was (1) generous, (2) open to new ideas, and (3) courageous. I've touched on these three characteristics only briefly so I would have time to say more about a fourth characteristic: He encouraged others, accepted them; he could see their potential; in other words, he saw people with the eyes of the Christ.

... I need a Barnabas in my life every day, don't you? In fact, I need several! And they often appear—but not always! And I need to be a Barnabas every day, but I'm not! Therefore, I decided to start a club—the "Barnabas Club." The Alpha Chapter was started in 1991 at First UMC in Kenosha, when I first preached about Barnabas. I mentioned that 1991 sermon (Invitation to Join the Barnabas Club) because it leads into a story.

I retired in 2000 after serving the Kenosha church for eleven years. Then, in 2004 I was asked to come back for a church banquet. The event was the kick-off for their fall financial drive. I was told that they wanted me to sing with a group providing entertainment for the event.

Well, they didn't really need me to sing; they wanted me there to receive a plaque announcing that a room in the church was now called "The Charles F. Bauer-King Room."

The M.C. that evening was a man named Dick Prince ... At the close of the presentation of this plaque to me, Dick reached for his billfold and showed me and others his Barnabas Club membership card! He had been carrying it for the past thirteen years. Wow! That got to me for indeed he had been a Barnabas—an encourager—to me, to many in the congregation, and to many in the Kenosha community ...

... Well, today you should have already received your Barnabas Membership Card. And repeating what I said twenty years ago (and have said a couple of other times in other churches),

> *What you do with it is up to you. Membership in this club will only be known as—in the days, weeks, months, and years to come—the characteristics of Barnabas are revealed ... through us to others one by one.*

[Nancy]

Ah, Charlie. When you preached this, did I ask you if there was a Barbara Club? Can't *women* promise to be generous, open-minded, courageous, and encouraging? Though you aren't here to answer, I can see you grin and add a paragraph or two to include women.

Or to satisfy me.

You evidently preached this club invitation other times, but I only heard it once and the 2011 sermon is the only copy I have. Four membership cards are attached—by a rusty paper clip.

MEMBERSHIP CARD: THE BARNABAS CLUB

This certifies that I _____ have chosen to be a member of The Barnabas Club.

Like Barnabas - early Christian leader, companion of Paul, sponsor of John Mark -

I have committed myself to
- *Openness to new ideas
- *Generosity
- *Courageous living
- *Encouraging others

I will regularly ask God for the love and strength necessary to maintain this membership commitment.

Signed _____ Date _____
(valid through: all of life)

Curious to see if this was the last time you invited folks to join the club, I went to your Pastoral Record book and discovered you preached 81 more times before you died, but no more Barnabases (Barnabi?) were listed.

More important to me than joining another club is the story you told about Dick. His witness was tangible evidence of the positive impact of your ministry with him. I remember your surprise at the gifts given and grateful response to Dick and the community of faith you had served through a major renovation.

In my experience, such affirmations were rare and most often shown or shared with me as I was leaving a church for a new appointment in another parish.

Years before I gave any thought to seminary, a pastor had said, "Nancy, you aren't aware of the power you have." I had no clue what he was talking about. However, after a short time as pastor, I began to understand. People who listened to me in meetings and personal conversations as well as sermons often heard things differently than what I intended. My word seeds sometimes took root and grew into troubled plants as well as a few sweet-smelling flowers. Your story reminds me I often do not know the impact of my words.

I recently read power described in two ways: power which dominates or oppresses and power which persuades and attracts. Words of encouragement—ala Barnabas—definitely attract. I think of the thirty years of encouragement you gave me.

I hold you in my heart, my love.

Disciples Are Called
Matthew 1.14–20
First UMC, Kenosha (1/16/1994)

[Charlie]
... I made my decision to study for the ministry in the summer between my sophomore and junior years of high school. I signed a decision card indicating that as my intention at an early morning communion service which was preceded by a consecration service the night before. The place was our Cincinnati

district Methodist Senior High Camp. That night before the communion service, I got little sleep as I spent the time in prayer and in conversation about my life with my pastor, George Taylor. He was at camp that summer as a counselor. Later, looking back on that event, I saw how God used Reverend Taylor and guided his words to me through that night. It was how I was called into the ordained ministry.

Reverend Taylor felt that the life altering decision I had made should be shared with our church—a congregation of about five hundred. And so, in November, 1952 I preached my first sermon. I called it "The Borrowing Christ." My text was from the Sermon on the Mount: "Give to everyone who begs from you, and do not refuse anyone who wants to borrow from you." I realize today that I pulled that verse out of context; nevertheless, the fact I was trying to convey then is still true, namely that Jesus wants to borrow us, take our lives and use them for his service …

The call that I experienced nearly forty-two years ago is still real, my enthusiasm is as great as it ever was, and most weekends I just can't wait to start the service. Now, there are frustrations and disappointments, of course, but the opportunities I have had and expect to have for several years more certainly overcome the occasional feelings of defeat. Never in those years have I felt abandoned by God or that I made the wrong decision.

[Nancy]

Charlie, I can understand your comment about not feeling abandoned by God, but questioning your decision about ordination? Really? You never questioned your decision? Never? Early in our relationship you told me about the significant conversation you had with Reverend Taylor. For you at sixteen-years-old, the call was clear. But I am still amazed that you never wavered in your commitment.

You've heard my struggle with "call." Just the opposite of yours. Junior High Church Camp. Thursday Night Consecration Service. I'm one of 150 kids sitting on the grass in front of a looming cross lit by a crackling fire and listening to a ten-foot-tall at least pastor with a soothing lisp invite us to give our lives to Jesus. We could indicate our commitment by standing up, or walking part way toward the cross, or we could give our whole life by coming all the way to the cross. I went "all the way" with Jesus.

To those of us with faces glowing and fervent with firelight zeal, the pastor said, "You may be wondering what giving your life to Jesus means. Boys, you may become pastors. Girls, you may become a pastor's wife."

Years later I caught on to the gender trick, but at the time women couldn't be fully ordained elders in the Methodist Episcopal Church. I also saw the image of my pastor's wife, her corseted corpulence wearing a dress with a purple and orange paisley design that looked like flopping fish. Pastor's *wife*? No way.

But call? You end your sermon with a "call" to the congregation:

The Master has borrowed men and women's time, abilities, money and lives, but Jesus has always returned them greatly enriched, filled to overflowing... That has been my experience and this is an invitation to you to respond for the first time or answer the call once more as the Master approaches saying, "Follow me."

Only in these last few weeks have I even allowed Jesus to show up in my panoply of dead helpers and only because you brought him. Actually, I think Jesus is horrified at what the centuries have done to him.

Spirit, Water, and Blood
1 John 5.1–12
First UMC, Appleton (5/21/89)

[Charlie]

What concrete ways do you have of remembering who you are and who is your family? Sometimes my sorting and packing process gets slowed up as I come across a particular photograph, or a book I'm ready to throw out until I read the inscription inside, or a certain matchbook cover, or a diploma or pin or trophy or toys I found and saved from Cracker Jack boxes over forty years ago. Memories in the head don't do it alone for us; we also need the tangible—the pennant, the dance card, the license plate, the bread and juice.

A preacher of a former generation made this point when he said, "I might pick a rosebud off a bush and it would be a rosebud and no more. But the one I love best in all the world might pluck a rosebud and give it to me, and it would be a rosebud and a great deal more. The substance would be changed because she gave it to me."

[Nancy]

Charlie, I read this paragraph while sitting on the love seat and immediately looked over at that pear-shaped ornament hanging from the mantle. The last gift you gave me. You didn't know who I was or remember buying it and I thought it was ugly, but like the old preacher's rosebud, that bauble is a great deal more than a few wires and plastic beads.

The ornament opens the story of you and your son at the Milwaukee Art Museum, bumping into Jane, who moved to North Carolina after Dick died. And Dick, who surprised you with his Barnabas card and by announcing that the new Great Room at Kenosha First UMC would be named after you.

Your sermon, of course, was about communion. The bread and wine (or grape juice in the UMC, thanks to prohibition and Mr. Welch's shrewd business sense) are the tangibles we're given to remember Jesus and his love.

Years before we met, I attended a weeklong workshop titled "The Body as a Means of Grace." The last day one of the leaders stood in front of me, looked at the caved-in dip at the base of my neck and said, "You will need several years of love from a man to become healed." I remember swallowing the strange words, knowing the man I was married to wasn't the one.

I don't take communion anymore. I don't believe the "Jesus loves me and died for me" atonement theology. But when I look at the mantle and see the very tangible gaudy ornament you bought me at the museum shop, I remember *your* healing love. A kind of presence with me that I don't understand, but am grateful for.

How to be Remembered
1 Thessalonians 1.1–10
First UMC, Kenosha (1/12/1997)

[Charlie]
Often when I meet with families following the death of a loved one, I ask them, "What do you remember about this person? What are the things you would like me to know about him or her?" Within the past two weeks two people who were important in my life have died—both wives of Wisconsin pastors. As I wrote letters to their husbands, I mentioned things that I remembered about them. That's what we do, isn't it? We

remember. And at such times the thought always crosses my mind: "I wonder what people will remember about me?"

One time I asked a church full of people to write out one or two things that they hoped people would remember about them. I collected the cards, read and organized them, and turned those responses into a sermon. Their replies fell into four categories: First, things that related to their faith and relationship to the Christ; second, some mentioned particular activities and skills—for example, "I'm a good musician;" third, some spoke of their relationships to others—family members, friends, animals; and fourth, quite a few folks listed virtues or characteristics—kind, friendly, loving, enthusiastic, and so on.

I mention all this today in preparation for the hearing of our lesson from 1 Thessalonians.

[Nancy]

Charlie, you wondered what people would remember about you? I went to the large box containing all the cards that arrived after your death. You would have counted them, of course, so that's what I did as I reread them. One hundred twenty-six cards with expressions of sympathy. Most of them included handwritten notes.

These remembrances of you were mentioned several times: great smile; kindness; best sermons; positive impact; twinkle in his eye; full of energy; good mentor.

Those are all true, of course. Here are a few more I particularly liked: faithful; empowering; smart, witty, and fun; bounced on his toes when he sang.

But my favorite: "He is still the only man I know to take his wife's name."

This makes me smile. Before we were married you listened to my concerns about my surname. We had long discussions about finding a new one that described our calling. I suggested Charles King and Nancy Queen, which went nowhere. Finally, we decided we liked the implied polarity of Bauer ("farmer" in German) and King. Our kids called us the Burger Kings.

Your sermon, of course, had very little to do with names or remembering. The scripture was to encourage early followers of Jesus to wait patiently until his return when they would be raised from the dead.

I don't believe in resurrection—at least of my physical body. But you came alive again as I read through that pile of sympathy cards.

Anger: One Letter Short of Danger
Matthew 5.21–24; Ephesians 9.25–26; James 1.19–20
First UMC, Kenosha (10/8/1995)

[Charlie]

On September 10, the *Chicago Tribune* published an article titled: "The Fires Within: Anger, the Sixth Deadly Sin." Well, this week that's our topic: Anger. Add the letter "D" and you get Danger.

Somewhere early in my life I started making a distinction between being irritated and being angry. To be irritated was okay; to be angry was *not* okay. My wife says she often can't tell the difference between my irritation and my anger, but there really *is* a difference *to me*… it has to do with the intensity of my emotions and what they are directed at. The issue is not, do we get angry, but rather it's when we get angry. What touches us off? How does our anger get expressed? Or maybe your anger doesn't get expressed.

This *Tribune* article generalizes about the difference between men and women saying that when men get mad, they could steam vegetables with the heat of their rage. Men act out their anger, and women tend to absorb theirs. Some use their mouth to shout, blame and insult when angry; others use their angry mouths to overeat. Whatever expression it may take, we are affected by anger—ours and others.

Affected by anger, yes. But is anger really a sin at all …?

[Nancy]

Oh Charlie. This is hard. I don't know where you are, if you can read these words or even intuit my thoughts. Yes. Anger. While we were together, you used words like irritated, annoyed, or frustrated to indicate your anger. You didn't attack verbally or physically. So, I have to believe the dementia caused your volatile behavior and you didn't know what you were doing when you threw coffee, kicked, and locked me out of the condo. And now, I want—no, I *need*—to tell you about the night you dug your fingernails into my wrist and drew blood.

The evening began unraveling when a sudden blast of wind blew a lounge chair off the deck. Within minutes rain flew sideways past our windows and an hour later, the 24/7 *Home Instead* woman, four neighbors and I were in the basement fighting a flood with a shop vac, mops, rags, and brooms. I came up from the basement to check on you and saw you pushing a sopping mop across the living room floor. Charlie. I know somewhere in your tattered sponge of a brain you thought you were helping, but instead of wresting the mop from you, I ended up applying bandaids to my wrist. It hurt.

Your sermon didn't mention *hurt* as an underlay of anger. My physical injury healed in a couple days, but the emotional hurts are woven into the fabric of those last months of your life. And mine.

Happy Are the Sad
Matthew 5.4
Trinity UMC, Racine (2/20/1972)

[Charlie]

Each beatitude of Jesus tells how life with God reverses the obvious. Each statement makes us readjust our thinking, or at least that is the intention. It is surely true with today's saying: "Blessed are they that mourn." This is telling us: "Happy are those who are sad," Or, in the Phillips translation, which conveys real meaning to me: "How happy are those who know what sorrow means…"

Now how can one be happy when one is sad? To ask that question may cause us to miss the point altogether. Regardless of what else he intended the Master at least meant this: one cannot have the possibility of being happy unless he also has the possibility of being sad. Mourning is the penalty we pay for living. We are capable of sorrow because we care. If we would eliminate all sorrow from life, then we must eliminate all love …

I believe that the key to understanding this most paradoxical of all Beatitudes is to identify the sad mourners. Who are they? Well certainly the Beatitude should be taken literally: the mourners are people like many of you, who have known personal loss through death or perhaps fire or accident. At this point, I have to speak of "you." I can't talk about "us" for I haven't yet experienced the heart-rending tragedies that eventually are inevitable to all. But I have been a pastor long enough to have gained some empathy and insight. And I know that sorrow can show us, as nothing else can, the kindness and love of our fellowmen; and it also can show us as nothing else can that depth of the comfort and compassion of God.

[Nancy]

Charlie, you were 35-years-old when you preached this sermon. I think your parents were still alive, your sister was still speaking to you, and your wife and three children were bright, creative, and healthy.

At 84-years-old, you had survived broken bones, surgeries, cancer, deaths of your parents and your sister, but never the death of a spouse.

While I agree with you to live a full life includes a wide range of emotions, I don't like the "happy are those who are sad" translation. I don't even like the New Revised Standard's "Blessed are those who mourn" or the rest of the verse, "for they shall receive comfort."

I look for comfort. I read the daily selection from *Healing After Loss* every morning. I talk with two widowed friends over tea. I meditate. I put your picture on my iMac's wallpaper—or whatever that background is called. You are standing above the roiling waters in Cascais, in your blue and gray striped knit shirt and a broad smile. As always, 3 x 5 cards and a pen are in your shirt pocket, readily available for you to write down a name, a place, a time. Every time I put the computer to sleep, I look into your sun-squinted blue eyes and say "I love you, Charlie. Goodbye."

Yes. I am grateful for people who listen, bring me soup, and invite me to their home for supper with fully vaccinated and boosted friends. But "happy" or "blessed" because I mourn?

I have moments when simply wanting to be alive is a challenge.

The Surprising Advent
Luke 1.5–25, 57–66
Oconomowoc UMC (12/17/78)

[Charlie]

Do you know how to make me nervous and somewhat fearful? It's quite easy. Here are the magic words that do it every time: "Now, let's break into small groups."

I know that more learning can take place through the interchange that happens between people in small groups, but you cannot remain anonymous in a group of three or four. You are on the spot. There is a tension which sometimes turns out to be quite creative, but I don't like it anyway. I thought of that yesterday when I was reflecting on Zechariah's fear. He is suddenly one-on-one with God's messenger! Questions get asked and answers are expected.

But the description of the experience does not end with fear. "Be not afraid," the angel said to him. "Do not be afraid," said the angel to Mary. "Be not afraid …"

[Nancy]

My homiletics prof said, "We preach what we most need to hear." In 1978 you evidently needed to hear "Don't be afraid, Charlie. Don't be afraid of small groups."

You expressed your fear to me privately during one of those mandatory clergy workshops. Was it the Myers Briggs? The clergy sexual abuse? The latest promotional gimmick? Uncomfortable, you nevertheless participated and even used the method in many of the classes you taught. However, you continued to be more self-revealing in your sermons than you were in conversations with our friends. Oh, you readily shared opinions, brandished your ACLU card, and stood with me to support the women trying to enter the Fox Valley Reproductive

Center, but you listened and asked questions more than you revealed personal issues.

Yet, it was your questioning and careful listening to my fears that helped me when a group of people in one of the churches wanted me gone because of my gender. "We've already had our woman," one man said, referring to the woman who preceded me in that parish. Like that congregation had already sacrificed enough.

I could learn better administrative skills, and learn better preaching methods, but I couldn't change my gender. You helped me learn I would survive the searing wash of naked vulnerability.

Thank you.

What Shall I Do With Jesus?
Mark 15.6–15
Trinity UMC, Racine (3/24/74)

[Charlie]

What shall I do with Jesus? It is the question no one of us can avoid. Pilate could not get away from it. He *had* to do something about Jesus. And so do we! The crowd had a simple answer to the question. "Crucify him, reject his claim to kingly power." There are other alternatives for us, and all but one are equally as destructive. But the disciples' answer was to surrender and obediently follow their Master. And once that decision was made concerning what *they* would do with Jesus, then they discovered Jesus the Christ saying to them "Here's what I want to do with *you!*"

[Nancy]

Eeeeuw. The words you put in Jesus' mouth are terrible. I see my former spouse gripping my wrists together and pushing me onto the bed. Completely trapped. No escape from what he wanted to do *to* (not *with*) me.

But until recently the question—What shall I do with Jesus?—bounced around like pin balls in my brain. Frankly I don't know what to do with Jesus these days. Mostly my answer is "Jesus was a great teacher. So was Buddha. So is the Dalai Lama, Thich Naht Hahn, and Annie Dillard."

If you were alive, still cognizant, and calling Jesus "Master," how would you respond to my answer?

I know you preached this during Lent—the liturgical season during which good church folks are supposed to reflect on their own faithfulness. This is Holy Week. I'm opting out of the story. It always turns out the same and, it's Jesus' integrity that got him killed, not some cosmic puppeteer.

While I don't like your question, I do believe questions are the edges of growth.

What does the world need? What do I enjoy doing? When the answers converge, that's my clue for an active response.

What do I enjoy doing? At the moment, dancing my fingers across a keyboard.

What does the world need? The needs of the world feel like a bottomless pit. I have no idea how to help.

What About Life After Death?
Portions of 1 Corinthians 15
First UMC, Kenosha (10/30/1994)

[Charlie]
Look what I found in my file folder marked "Death and Immortality." It's a copy of a headline from the November 8, 1983 *Star*—that tabloid you read while standing in line to check out your groceries. "New Proof of Life after Death, 7-year-old girl's story stuns doctors." But that's all there is—it's a copy of the original; the rest of the story is missing and I don't know how I acquired this. I do know that I didn't buy the newspaper. But a lot of people did, and do. After all, people with inquiring minds want to know about everlasting life—so they buy the *Enquirer* or the *Star*. I think it would be a lot more helpful if they would read the 15th chapter of Pauls' first letter to the Corinthian Church.

... The thing most often said—by Christians and non-Christians alike—is that human life is divided into two parts: there's the life of the body and the life of the soul; the life of the body ends in death, but the soul is immortal—it lives on forever.

... Now you are free to believe anything you want to, whether it comes from the pen of Shirley McLaine or the mouth of some Eastern maharishi. I just don't want anyone to call this idea that a person's body dies and the soul inevitably lives on "Christian." You see, the Bible doesn't teach that—anywhere! I've said this before in sermons, classes, and conversations and I've discovered that people get angry; they feel threatened. And yet the idea of separate souls and bodies was something taught by Greek philosophers both before and during the decades of the early church's expansion. It was not a Christian teaching. In fact, some of the New Testament writings specifically speak out against this heresy.

[Nancy]

Whoa! You tackled the thorny topic of the soul. I don't remember you commenting on any repercussions. People in churches I served were mostly angry at the trustees' choice of carpet color for the lounge or how much to charge for the beef dinner.

Last Sunday I was one of a dozen people responding to a video expounding on a scripture quote attributed to Jesus: "throw him into the darkness, where there will be weeping and gnashing of teeth." No one seemed interested in the scholar's information about the context, the author's objective, or associations with current "hells." For 45 minutes, the conversation focused on what happens to our "souls" in an afterlife, being saved in an altar call, out-of-body experiences, and messages from a recently departed loved one.

I kept my mouth shut. I didn't want to say I have no idea if there is an afterlife. Nor did I say "The Soul isn't in my body. My body is in the Soul."

Charlie. I believe we are together somehow in that Soul.

Heavenly Worship
Isaiah 6.1–3; Revelation 4–5 (selections)
First UMC, Kenosha (4/25/1999)

[Charlie]

Last Sunday my wife and I were in Texas. We had just finished a week at an Elderhostel in Port Aransas which was run by the Marine Science Institute of the University of Texas. For me the highlight of the week was not the bird watching or the wild flower study, it was the day we went out on one of the University's marine research ships. On two occasions a net was lowered from the back of the boat and for several minutes it scraped up items from the bottom of the gulf. Then came the excitement as it was hauled to the boat and emptied out. "What did we get?" Our eagerness to know was tempered with a bit of tension as the professor dug into the seaweed. Suddenly some crabs headed toward us and a few jelly fish fell out of the net along with a sting ray. Eventually an eel, hermit crabs, and more than a dozen varieties of fish came forth. And even though I was on vacation, my preacher's mind was still working. Ah, if only worship could always carry with it this same sense of expectancy and awe, and even a bit of fear as we ask, "What might happen today? What discoveries will there be? Will the door of heaven be opened?"

[Nancy]
     Oh Charlie. The door to which you refer in this sermon is from the book of Revelation: "There in heaven a door stood open." But the "door" that flew open in my mind is not the one to heaven. It's the door to hell that I go through when I remember the night you escaped from Shorelight's Memory Care.
     Someone named Wendy calls at 8:40 p.m.
     "Has Charlie called in the last half hour?"
     "No?" *What? What happened?*
     "He's gone! He got out!"
     "How!?" *Oh God!*
     "We don't know. A back door?"
     I'm stunned into silence. Helpless. I see you wandering. Lost. Near the Lake. You started calling that morning at 8:30. I told you I couldn't come see you. I told you that you needed to stay there. You called 22 more times in the next hour and a half. I

counted. I quit answering after the fourth call. I listened to your voicemail messages.

You said, "Hello. Does my mother know I'm here? Does my wife?"

"Hello. I don't like it here. I don't like it one bit."

"Hello. I can be home in 15 minutes."

"Hello. This is your dad calling."

"Hello. This is Pastor Charles. You can reach me at 700 Waters Edge #5."

"Hello. I hope I'm reaching one of you. I love you all so very, very, much."

Then the last call. "I'm going to disappear!"

The Lake. Oh no. Lake Michigan. Waves. Crashing. Slapping against the rocks.

Into my rising panic, I hear Wendy speculating about an alarm that must not have worked … some door he must have found and … she interrupts herself and yells, "They found him!"

"Where?"

"Olympia Brown? Is that a place?"

"Yes." *Is that weak sigh of relief mine?* "Yes. A school. Just a block away."

The next morning, Angela, one of the nurses, called to tell me how you got out. You watched how people entered and left the Memory Care Unit, held a button down on a door, found steps to the first floor, and discovered the door to the parking lot —the only door in the facility that didn't have a key pad.

"He is smart," Angela said, "and fast. I've never seen anyone Charlie's age with so much energy. He's been awake for 48 hours."

Sweetheart. I lie awake haunted by the image of you hurrying home – and *almost* arriving. You. Almost home.

Home.

Home.

How I wish I would have run out, taken you by the hand and brought you home again.

Opened the door to heaven for you.

We Are Surrounded
Portions of Hebrews 11 and 12
First UMC, Kenosha (1/9/1994)

[Charlie]

Did you ever feel so low that you had to reach up to touch bottom? Well, when we get down and feel despair, we can gain encouragement from the great group of those who went before us. The communion of saints means that there is no real line separating us from those who have preceded us in death. Dozens of people have told me of the strength and encouragement and guidance they have felt from their spouse who had died: their parents; or some other important individual in their life. It was as though, it is as though, in the moment of loneliness and fear and indecision, that person's presence was very real. The grieving one was surrounded by love and by one who really *did* understand what was going on.

[Nancy]

Feel low? Charlie, you've been dead 19 months. The word *low* doesn't describe my experience. I might be walking along tangled in my own thoughts when out of nowhere I'm ambushed by something that reminds me of you. I couldn't sing a note of the opening hymn last Sunday. "Come Thou Fount of Every Blessing?" I could only see you at my right side, our shared grin during the second verse: *Here I raise mine Ebenezer, hither by thy help I'm come.*

Our grin was a smug grin because we were sure most of the worshipers were probably thinking of Scrooge and didn't know the Hebrew "ebhen ha-ezer" meant "Stone of Help" and referred to a rock Samuel picked up to thank his god for the victory against the Philistines.

Charlie, while the people were singing, I left the sanctuary, went into that little bathroom off the office, sat on the wooden toilet seat lid, took my mask off, and cried.

The topic of this sermon is the communion of saints. Saints—not perfect persons, but the mystical body of all those alive or dead that have been born through baptism into some kind of eternal life.

For the past forty years, in times of fear and indecision, you and my friend, Rusty, not some dead saints, were the ones who encouraged me, comforted me, and helped guide me. You are both dead.

And you say dozens of people told you they'd been helped by someone close to them who has died. I call on you. I beg you to answer. I look from this desk to the doorway and long to see you there leaning against the frame watching me. You are not there.

What about the communion of saints? Where are *they*?

There was the night my grandmother and her sisters joined me in the hot tub. I had come home from a meeting during which I had to respond to a group that had formed in the congregation requesting that the bishop appoint me somewhere else. For several days you had listened to my distress. You were already in bed and asleep when I came in the back door. I didn't want to wake you. I crept into the family room, and lowered myself into the comforting water. Light from the moon burst through the window into the room and lit up the pastel painting my Great Aunt Grace had rendered over a hundred years ago. Cows standing underneath trees at the edge of a stream in the setting sun. Grace, Myrtie, and Inez joined me in the amniotic fluid and listened. An hour later, I was back in bed next to you, asleep. Good thing we had a hot tub then that held four people easily.

Charlie, in your moments of fear and confusion, I hope you were cared for by saintly staff people. I'm still devastated that some fuzzy gumball of a virus kept me from being with you. I hope upon hope that some of those old dead saints showed up to comfort you. Your mother. Your dad. Maybe even Rusty.

Enter God: Into Old Age
Isaiah 46.3–4; Psalm 92.1–4, 12-15; 2 Corinthians 4.16–5.2
First UMC, Kenosha (3/29/1992)

[Charlie]

I was twenty-seven years old and in my second year as pastor of the La Paz Community Church in Bolivia when Mrs. Jimmy Cook said to me, "You know, Charles, when the vote was taken to call you to this church, I spoke up and said, 'but he's so young; what does he know about sin?' but listening to you I've discovered that you know quite a bit about sin."

Well, I didn't really, but I read a good deal, and I was beginning to be exposed to people's experiences through pastoral counseling. Yes, I talked a lot about sin and the raising of children, marriage, communications, forgiveness, and many other things without having had much personal first-hand experience. I was probably like a priest with whom I once shared a wedding. The priest gave the homily—a beautiful message to the bride and groom about the nature of love, but it was so theoretical and ethereal and lacked any "I have lived it" practicality.

All that took longer to say than I intended. I just wanted to get across the fact that in my opinion I'm not old, and so I've approached the preparation of this message with a good deal of trepidation and dependence on statements by others. Therefore, if I take up the subject again in twenty years when I get to seventy-five, I may have something entirely different to say.

[Nancy]

As far as I know, Charlie, you didn't preach about old age again and what you said in the seven pages of this sermon was entirely dependent upon others. You listed negatives (bad jokes, songs, stereotypes, terminology) and positives (redefining one's status, freed-up energy to use, living in the present). You spoke about aging as a spiritual adventure. Like the priest to which you alluded in the opening of this sermon, you did not include any personal experiences, because you didn't consider yourself old.

But at seventy-five? And eighty? You still acted young. You helped with worship every Sunday at Wauwatosa Avenue, preached once a month, led a couple classes, and made pastoral calls to shut-ins and the hospitalized. You literally ran up the church steps. Because you took only one pill a day (to my handful), I was convinced I would die years before you.

At the end of this sermon, you quote the psalmist and challenge the congregation to care for the elderly. *Do not cast me off in the time of old age; do not forsake me when my strength is absent.*

Forsaken. The word forsaken is searing. I felt such relief the day I took you to Shorelight Memory Care. For the first time in months, I slept without waking every time you moved. While you were home you had been so active. You kept leaving the house. You tried starting the car with the house key. You lit a fire under the electric pot. You used the kitchen chair for your toilet. The invasion of Covid-19 meant the help from *Home Instead* quit coming.

What real hope I had as I left you at Shorelight. Certainly, the virus would not last and in a week or two I would be permitted to be with you.

Four months and three facilities later, Burr Oak called to say I could come the next day. You died before I got there.

Forsaken. The word cuts clean.

You were forsaken. By me.

Amazement
John 2.1–12
First UMC, Kenosha (2/23/1997)

[Charlie]

Last Sunday evening my wife returned from a weekend retreat in Michigan. I heard her drive into the garage, heard the trunk of the car open, and then heard the sound of breaking glass. She had returned with a bottle of wine which broke through the bottom of the bag. In spite of our efforts, the smell lingered for several days. "I wish the wine would turn to water," I said at one point using the preacher's gift of finding sermon illustrations in almost every event.

[Nancy]

I *love* this, Charlie. I had forgotten about the crash. You probably heard a loud *Damn it!* which, of course, you didn't include. By mentioning wine you risked the disapproval of the few disciplined United Methodists who still abstained from alcohol. You should have thanked me for providing you with that great line, a good opening illustration for this sermon.

You were preaching a series on Jesus' miracles and cautioned listeners not to get caught up trying to figure out how it happened, or whether it happened, but *why* the story was told.

You claimed the gospel writer wanted us to see that *whenever* Jesus enters the scene, there is a new quality of life—at that moment. You used the words sparkling, exciting, thrilling.

Like fine wine.

These days I try to find comfort in remembering some of our sparkling moments: the hot air balloon ride, the crest of Huayna Picchu, our drive across the state to get a piece of pie at the Norske Nook. But those times are overshadowed by your hands trying to reach me through the window of Azura Memory Care and your open gape-mouthed face of death.

Our Fathers Who Are on Earth
Colossians 3.12–21, 23–24
Trinity UMC, Racine (5/5/1974)

[Charlie]

No one ever talks very much about Father's Day. It shows up on the calendar there in June and catches us by surprise. About the only ones who make us aware of it are the merchants who want to use the occasion to clear out their stock of slippers, pipes, fishing equipment, golf ball washers, tools, and ties. Perhaps it's only our sense of fair play that causes us to have a

Father's Day at all. Mom has her day and just so Dad won't feel left out we'll also have one for him.

I must admit that in my fifteen years of preaching ministry I've never ever presented a Father's Day sermon. Sometimes I was on vacation in June when the date came up; often I would throw in a paragraph or two about the importance of Father in my Mother's Day message and let it go at that; or perhaps the knowledge that I was still learning a lot about being a father led me to skip the subject. Or—here's another thought—maybe Father's Day gets glossed over in church because we don't naturally associate Father with the church.

… All this is too bad, and so a few months ago I decided that, this year at least, I'd talk about our fathers who are on earth in May—and before we honor the mothers.

[Nancy]

Oh my God, Charlie! You told me about getting into trouble after you preached this, but I hadn't seen it. I read every judgmental, sexist and outdated-world-view word, wincing through all the oily oughts and shoulds about being a good father. You never did honor the mothers, who were there hoping to hear words of admiration, honor, and praise for all the sacrifices they had made—just like Jesus. No wonder they were pissed. Their kids, too, probably dragged to worship only to please mom and afterward finding themselves faced with her wilting-corsage anger.

What karma led me to find this today, of all days? You preached this on May 5. I found it today, May 5. And if you were still alive, we would be going to Blue Sombrero to celebrate our 32nd Cinco de Mayo anniversary.

"I never made *that* mistake again," you said, after telling me the story of your apostasy. I found references in subsequent sermons that indicated you were still embarrassed decades later:

December 10, 1995: It was May, 1974 and I was pastor in Racine when I made the terrible mistake of miscalculation ...

December 23, 2007: On May 5, 1974, I was a very unpopular preacher ...

Every Mother's Day—forever after—you chose women from the Bible or United Methodist history to illustrate characteristics of a "Good Mother." You wisely saved your sermons about "Good Fathers" for Advent, when everyone seemed okay to hear about Joseph.

But you as a father? Your pride in your children and their successes was palpable. Yet, your reflections of yourself as a father were filled with regrets at not being more accessible as they were growing up.

Faith and Fundamentalism
Scripture sentences
Oconomowoc, UMC (3/1/1981)

[Charlie]

... I had several other things in my original outline for this sermon, but they were in a descending order of importance and I'm running out of time. And I want to save the remaining moments to say this: There are some good things about fundamentalism: The fundamentalist should be admired for his insistence on personal Christian experience, for her dedication to Jesus and her attempts to make Jesus the Lord of her life; the fundamentalist should be admired for his willingness to be courageously different from his society because of his faith. At its best the religion of fundamentalists has led people to a deep personal devotion in which saintliness is not uncommon and the paramount demands of the Gospel are humbly recognized.

And if there are people here today who hold to the fundamentalist position, I want to say that I welcome you in Christian love and fellowship; we are glad that you are here. United Methodism is a pluralistic faith which embraces Christians of both liberal and conservative thought, for each person is urged to work through his and her own faith based on a study of the Scriptures, Church history, the arguments of reason, and ultimately what the Holy Spirit leads us to experience and validate. That search, that study, leads people to different points of view and that's good, for as we dialogue and share our ideas we grow stronger in our faith.

And so I state unequivocally that we believe fundamentalists are our brothers and sisters in Christ. We need to know and understand them better, and we pray that they will, in turn seek to be more open in understanding us that we may grow together in Christ.

[Nancy]

Oh my. Would you preach this again, Charlie? These last paragraphs seem so naïve, as if any dialogue between Christian liberals and conservatives is still possible. Also, strongly implied throughout your sermon is an "us and them" dichotomy, which drips arrogance. Yet, as you stated at the onset, this topic was in response to a request and your four-paged, single-spaced discourse, which included historical background, definitions, and comparisons, was a well-reasoned answer. But, rather than "Good News," this sermon feels like a lecture.

I'm curious about the scripture sentences you chose. The selections didn't appear in your sermon and weren't printed in the bulletin. At least you used the him and her pronouns.

Even while you were losing touch with "reality," (whatever *that* is), you were aware our denomination is in the process of splitting. So much for the pluralistic embrace of liberal and conservative you espouse. While the cause of the schism is purported to be over the ordination of our LGBTQA+ kin, there are underlying liberal and conservative theological issues which boil down to arguments about God.

If asked to preach on this issue, I wonder what I would say. Maybe something about hope. I like the quote by Joan Chittester: *Hope is the hardest love we carry.*

I keep hoping.

Lydia
John 14. 23–29; Acts 16.11–15
Little Prairie UMC (5/16/2004)

[Charlie]
    … Nearly forty years ago my family and I took an extensive vacation. We were living in Bolivia and planned a three-week trip to Argentina, Uruguay, and Chile. Now I had written ahead to pastors in those countries for information about inexpensive lodging. As a result, we spent time in a seminary dormitory in Buenos Aires and in an Anglican guesthouse in Santiago, Chile. But when we arrived in Montevideo, Uruguay I discovered that the term "inexpensive" did not mean the same thing to the minister who made the arrangements, as it did to me. I cancelled the reservation in the resort hotel and found us a 50 cent per person per night hotel—cheap, but very inadequate to say the least.

Then we met two British folks who had settled in Uruguay. They found us lodging in a home, took us out to eat, to a park, and gave us an extensive tour of the city. Once I asked them why they were doing all this for us. Their answer was simple: "The Bible tells us to. It says, 'Do not neglect to show hospitality to strangers.'"

[Nancy]

Charlie, I know your sermon was about Lydia, a wealthy woman and early Christian leader, who showed hospitality. And also your mom's name. But if you are present in some form as I'm writing these responses, you already know why I chose these paragraphs because I was reminded of those terrible "inexpensive" lodgings.

When we traveled by car, you picked up booklets at all the rest stops and found the "best" deals. We stayed in motels with broken lights, cigarette burns in the bedspread, pubic hair on the "clean" sheets. There was the manager in Wyoming who apologized about no air-conditioning, but was kind enough to give us a can of beans to hold the window up if we wanted it open. And how about our frantic commotion in that motel near the San Francisco airport, the only non-smoking room available with only one key—the master key—held by the owner, who promised we could go out for an early breakfast and he would be available to let us back in.

He wasn't.

You rang his bell. Woke up his wife who said he had to take his father to the hospital and must have taken the key with him. You took off the screen, crawled in, and got our luggage. We made it to the airport on time.

After several Grand Circle trips and five-star hotels, you became more amenable to an occasional Holiday Inn, but I realize now those sterile accommodations didn't give us the best stories. Endearing stories that make me smile.

Mostly because of your early frugality, my deference, and our agreed-upon values we were financially able to live our retirement years in this beautiful condo.

I am so grateful.

Sometimes I sense you standing next to me. Looking out at the lake.

Stop, or Go?
Luke 10.25–37
Wauwatosa Avenue UMC (7/11/2010)

[Charlie]
 Several times a week I'll start to tell my wife, Nancy, about some event in my past. But after more than twenty years of marriage I've learned to ask, "Have you heard this story before?" And she often replies, "Yes, four or five times already." She knew what was coming! That must be how many of you reacted when you learned that today's scripture from Luke concerns "The Good Samaritan." You know what's coming so you can disengage. At least that's what I tend to do when I'm listening to some preacher deal with an old familiar story. But then he or she will often suddenly say something new, exciting, relevant and I'm involved. Maybe that can happen today.

[Nancy]
 Charlie, did I ever compliment you on your creativity? In one sermon you gave answers, then questions like Jeopardy. In another you played Johnny Carson's "Carnak the Magnificent"

with answers in envelopes. After we saw *Shear Madness* you had the congregation vote on one of two endings. Several times you did character sketches and turned parables into plays or dialogs.

To keep people engaged in the Good Samaritan story, you found a drama in a reader's script for four-voices and adapted it into a fast-moving dialogue that you did with the lead pastor. I read through the play this morning and am sure most folks were attentive.

But it's neither the Good Samaritan story nor your creativity that evokes my response. I want to comment about sharing stories with each other, which, after all, is what good sermons do. This morning's calendar quote was the prompt:

> *The pleasure of remembering had been taken from me, because there was no longer anyone to remember with. It felt like losing your co-rememberer meant losing the memory itself, as if the things we'd done were less real and important than they had been hours before.*
>
> ~ John Green, *The Fault in our Stars*

Charlie. I have friends with whom I share stories about you. Stories about your creativity, your kindness, frugality, impatience, and your need to have a green vegetable every night as part of your dinner. So far, I haven't lost those memories, but since your death the stories seem less important. More than that, I realize we've already made all the memories together we're ever going to make. I will never have any new stories to share about you.

I remember Kaye. At her daughter's funeral, she said, "I have lots of memories left. I'm going to wear every one of them out."

The memories I have with you? I don't want to wear *any* of them out.

God is Great!
Hosea (Selected)
First UMC, Appleton (1/13/1985)

[Charlie]

Last Sunday was, for some, a day of consciousness raising. I talked about how language can limit our thinking; and I was especially concerned with the issue of how we speak of God. I invited your questions and comments. I especially wanted to hear from persons who took exception to some of the things that I said, or what they *thought* I said; then this Sunday I could clarify or elaborate the issues that I raised. Well, I got a response—Sunday afternoon and throughout the week—many verbal comments as well as two letters. And with but one exception they were overwhelmingly, enthusiastically positive. And yet throughout the week I continued to hear second and third hand about people who weren't going to come back this Sunday and listen to any more of that kind of stuff.

[Nancy]

Oh Charlie ... you really lit a fire. The two sermons you preached expanding on the image of God stoked up so much heat that five days after this second sermon you made the Appleton *Post-Crescent*:

January 18, 1985

God: Father, Mother, Friend, Creator

... "God is neither male nor female. God is a spirit. Why do we think of 'him' as an elderly male parent in heaven," the Reverend Charles King wants to know.

... King, co-pastor of First United Methodist Church, an avowed feminist who has been passionate about desexing the language, felt that it's time people start accepting such changes even in liturgical terminology ..."

You made the newspaper, of course, not because your life had been threatened—it hadn't—but because someone who was aware of the controversial topic had alerted a reporter that you would be speaking at a "noon-hour philosophers" lecture series. Obviously, your radical (then) views were outed by the article and accompanying photograph.

At the time you were putting out the fires of your prophetic preaching, I was finishing my last year in seminary, renting a room at the home of Dr. Rosemary Radford Reuther, and steeped in her feminist theology. How pleasantly surprised I was during my Field Ed year at First Church to discover that you —a white male pastor—were not only up-to-date on current theological trends, but also incorporating your thinking into the life of the church.

Unfortunately, regarding "God" language, not much has changed in the liturgical rubrics.

I still attend worship on Sundays because my friends are there. We change the pronouns while singing the "hims."

Lent Us Pray
Luke 11.1–13
First UMC, Kenosha (2/14/1993)

[Charlie]
    I had been in the ministry for over twenty years when someone pointed out to me that I was saying "Lent us pray," instead of "Let us pray." Now old patterns and habits are hard to kill, and sometimes the wrong word still comes out of my mouth. Perhaps it's because I'm somewhat frightened or

intimidated when I pray out loud in public. I have this feeling that others do it so much "better."

This is a request sermon. A member asked if I would preach about prayer. And while I welcome and encourage all your sermon suggestions, I told the person that I had never preached a sermon about prayer that I was very satisfied with after it was over; but I would certainly attempt it once more. So, I spent some time the other day trying to get at the reasons for my feelings. I came up with a couple. For one thing I realized I have sometimes used examples of bad prayers—humorous ones and horrific ones ... Secondly, there is a problem with the format: I'm up here and you are there. It's an active-passive, talk-listen set up with sermons, but any talk about prayer suggests sharing, dialogue, responses, small groups. So let's take at least one small step toward that in this service. I would like us all to take a moment to complete a sentence for ourselves; then I hope you will feel comfortable enough to share your endings to the sentence with one another—with people near you. Here's the statement: "When I imagine the God to whom I pray, I think of ..."

[Nancy]

Gee, Charlie. What happened? Did people actually speak to one another? Did anyone comment about this to you on their way out of the service? And, did anyone ask *you* how *you* would fill in the blank? When you preached this sermon, we had been married almost three years and already had dozens of conversations about the word and concept "God." Though you agreed with me that God is ultimately Mystery and read all the latest scholarly wisdom, you said when you prayed, you imaged Jesus.

As I sifted through 60 years of your sermons, you raised the issue of God's image several times. Though you didn't argue with my heretical ideas, you were obviously influenced. I smiled when I found evidence.

God Who?
Psalm 34.1–6, 8–9; 1 John 3.13
Wauwatosa Avenue UMC (11/2/2014)

[Charlie]

If you start a conversation with my wife, Nancy, and speak about God, be warned. She may respond with this question: "God who?" That's what she used to ask me, interrupting me when I started talking about God. At first I didn't like the interruption. I thought she was trying to annoy me or tease me, but gradually I came to see the importance of that question. You see, the word "God" is tossed into so many of our sentences, but the meaning, the image, the expectations we have about God vary tremendously—and I think that's true today, more than ever.

[Nancy]

Oh Sweetheart. Almost 30 years passed between the 1985 news-making sermons about Mother God and this one. Your early sermons? More like lectures. But this one? You wisely and caringly built it on paradox and in doing so revealed the Holy cannot be named.

Last Sunday, people in the class after worship began talking about God's name: the I am who I am, YHWH, Jehovah, the Lord God Almighty, and on and on and on. I raised my arms up in front of me and said something like, "What do you call *this*

... this 'thing' we are sitting in here? This *moment*? Our presence in this presence?"

On Monday, I related the experience to Dwight-my-spirit-guide. He smiled and said, "Yes. Sometimes we get tired of trying to explain the mystery."

I sigh.

How I miss you.

In my next life (if there is one) I'm not going to ask questions. Ha!

The Woman Who Talked Back to Jesus
Matthew 15.21–28; 7.7–8
First UMC, Kenosha (8/5/1990)

[Charlie]

We don't have to recite the Apostle's Creed, or be able to explain the Doctrine of the Trinity, or believe in miracles, or

rust in our hearts. We simply come to
 we have exhausted all human
 our hands to him saying, "Have mercy
 which our Lord always responds—not
 :tion which results in: forgiveness,
 ıman relationships, insight, courage,
 our particular needs at this particular
 bring them with us as we celebrate the

 ;ermon series you preached on
women and also the first Sunday of the month—communion.

Rather than comment on the story of the woman at the well, "who talked back to Jesus," I want to tell you about the conversation I had with a church member who asked why I wasn't taking communion. I did my short answer. "When the guru points to the moon, the disciples don't look at the finger." She scrunched her forehead into confused wrinkles. I tried to explain. "In his stories and behavior, Jesus kept pointing to the Kingdom (or kin-dom) of God, which was already present. We look at Jesus-the-Finger and not the Mystery Moon with us. We've turned Jesus into an idol."

She shrugged, narrowed her eyes and didn't ask another question. She's probably going to tell someone I've given Jesus the finger.

What do I say to you now, my love? Even when you couldn't remember my name, you kept taking communion. Somehow you were fed by the "grain of life and grape of love" and you loved me in spite of my earlier assertion that Jesus died because of his integrity, not because of some sin I committed.

Do you remember Dwight? Maybe you already know I began meeting with him again after your death. Those days I felt swallowed whole into a deep maw of grief.

"I don't know what I believe any more about communion—or about Jesus," I said to Dwight last week. After listening for several minutes to my muddling, he said, "Well, *I* believe in the *archetype.*"

"Yes!" I laughed. "An archetype. I can believe in an archetype more easily than some guy who is never pictured with even a smudge on his Holy White outfit."

I googled Christ archetype. According to the framework of Carl Jung,

> *The self-revelation of God in Christ illustrates the way in which the problem of opposites arises when God becomes an object of conscious reflection.*

Ah. Charlie. When it came to theology, I don't remember much arguing with you. We looked beyond oppositional ideas, to the mystery moon of our love. But does Jung's idea about God in Christ mean I would be better off not reflecting on God at all? I suspect you would disagree with Jung and I would end up talking back to you. Like the woman at the well.

If You Lived in Antioch (1)
1 Peter 4.16; Acts 11.19–26
First UMC, Kenosha (5/29/1994)

[Charlie]
　… After thirty-five years in the ministry I've gotten used to having people react differently to me once they learn I'm a pastor; my wife, however, has been an ordained minister for only nine years and the contrasts are still fresh and sharp for her. "You're a reverend?" Suddenly language is cleaned up; certain jokes are censored; and there often is a kind of tentativeness in conversation as if we pastors will send down the wrath of God upon those who offend us. I don't like that! Should we not—all of us—be living each day with the continual awareness of Christ's Spirit with us; why does it take a pastor's presence to remind us of God?

[Nancy]
　Ah. I wondered if and when this ongoing issue would show up in one of your sermons. My immediate recollection was the night our friends, Patty and Greg, invited us to dinner. They wanted us to meet the Lawsons, their neighbors.

"Don't tell Bob and Louise what we do," I said to Patty, as we arrived at our friend's home.

"Why not?" Greg asked.

"Because the conversation will be stilted," you shrugged.

"Oh no. It won't." Greg argued.

"Yes it will," I said. "Trust me. There won't be any swearing. No dirty jokes."

"I don't believe it," Greg said, but he and Patty agreed to go along with our request. For almost an hour, the conversation between the six of us was easy and enjoyable. Here and there a four-letter word, a sexual innuendo, but *nothing* offensive or uncomfortable. Until ...

Bob asked, "What do you do, Charlie?"

"You mean work?"

Bob nodded.

"As little as possible." You grinned.

"Right, me too," Bob laughed, then added, "Do you work in Kenosha?"

"Yes."

"Where?"

"I have an office downtown."

"Where?"

"On Sheridan."

"*What?* What do you do?"

You confessed. Patty and Greg explained the subterfuge.

Was it our deception that caused a shift in the rest of the evening's exchange? More likely Bob and Louise had experienced pastors who thought *they* were God and were into rule keeping more than compassion. Or they may have had unexpressed expectations on their pastor that he or she didn't provide.

Like Mac, who accosted me before worship one Sunday.

"I'm angry at you," he said, shaking his index finger in my face. Mac, who after his retirement became the volunteer custodian, and found something almost every week to scold me for: a light left on after a meeting, the leaking toilet in the women's restroom, my intention to confirm the eighth graders, "who would *never* be back in church *ever* again."

I braced for another Mac Attack.

"My friend, Will, was in the hospital and you didn't visit."

"I didn't know Will was hospitalized," I shot back. "*No one* told me!"

Mac's bluster evaporated. He withdrew his reprimanding finger and bowed his head toward the carpet.

Aware of other people observing the interchange, I turned away. Only partially embarrassed of my defensiveness, I wanted to grab his crusty finger and jam it in his eye.

Now, even retired, I'm still uncomfortable about my role. People call me pastor. Do they expect something from me? What? I do not know what is expected of me and you are not here to listen.

If You Lived in Antioch (2)
1 Peter 4.16; Acts 11.19–26
First UMC, Kenosha (5/29/1994)

[Charlie]
    ... I know witness (of being filled with Spirit) could be made by countless individuals, including people right here who live with the certainty of the living presence of Jesus the Christ.

Should we not—all of us—be living each day with the continual awareness of Christ's Spirit?

[Nancy]
Yes. I'm still reflecting upon your Antioch sermon. After describing the tentative conversations that ensue when folks discover we're clergy, you say, "should we not—all of us—be living each day with the continual awareness of Christ's Spirit?"

I'm caught with the word *should*. Maybe folks are uncomfortable around clergy because they feel "should upon." Years of being hooked into guilt. Like my friend, Rusty, said, "Guilt—the gift that lasts forever."

Who wants to relate to people who represent a god that is only harsh, punitive, and demanding?

Your sermons from the 1960s and early 70s that survived the flooded basement are filled with black and white shoulds, advice, and your long lists of solutions for all kinds of distress. In the later 1970s I began to see a definite softening. Grays and colors showed up. Several times you confessed to your judgmentalism.

This morning's *Healing After Loss* meditation included a quote that referred to the distortion occurring if one only idealizes the person who has died. The author, Toby Talbot, wrote: *It's a betrayal to remember only the good parts.*

Not until the last four months of your life did I feel as if I had betrayed you. That was my behavior, not yours.

I do remember your flaws. Early in our marriage, you hollered at waitresses, were full of advice to your kids, and held off calling a plumber until the kitchen sink was completely clogged. Even after years of listening to my distress, you kept beeping at drivers in front of you who didn't see the light the second it turned green.

How is it that I miss your impatience, your hardline opinions, your shoulds as much as your smiles and love?

Jesus the Liberator
Isaiah 58.1–10; Luke 1.46–55
First UMC, Kenosha (12/8/91)

[Charlie]
   ... This summer the Village of Pleasant Prairie ran city water down our street and hooked us up to a copper water line installed when the house was built. But then, though the line was not connected to anything and simply came up through the basement floor, a construction worker turned the water on one morning so when I went home to fix supper there was eight inches of water on the floor and a three-foot-high geyser of water gushing from the unconnected pipe. Well, among the things destroyed was one box containing about twenty years of my old sermons. Now I could have dried out and saved some of them, but I chose to save only the paperclips. You see, a lot has changed in the world, in Biblical scholarship, and especially in my understanding of myself and you to whom I speak ...

   I've learned there are within all of us many layers of past
hu   ls; we carry around so
m   anxiety; you and I face
eı   ..
                               Jews—is this: Christ was
bc   lds us back from being all
th

[Nancy]

I remember that flood. After checking that we weren't going to get electrocuted, we hauled sopping stuff upstairs and spread clothing, books, and pictures all over the backyard to dry. Of course, your frugal nature necessitated saving the paper clips. If your words hadn't saved souls, at least something tangible was saved from all those sermons. And, now I understand the dearth of those earliest polemics. I'm glad most of them are gone.

As I went through boxes of your exhortations, I found evidence of dozens of those salvaged clips, rusty and leaving flaky imprints on page after page.

You might have found some use for them, but I threw them out.

We Heard That God is With You
Zechariah (selected)
First UMC, Kenosha (8/2/1998)

[Charlie]

One of the great joys and energizing things that happens to me is when a person in the church I serve decides to enter the ordained ministry. That's happened a number of times in the past, and in one case I received a paper that one of these pastors had written—reflecting on her first two years in the ministry. At the time she was serving three churches here in Wisconsin. She wrote, "Isn't a 'good' pastor supposed to help and love others, to do and be all things at all times? However, it did not take long for me to see that no matter how hard I tried, I would not be able to please or do all that they felt needed done ... The more I did, the more there came for me to do. If I did a good wedding or funeral, requests to do more arrived. The very things that affirmed me also added to my pain ..."

Well, after a period of self-examination, this new pastor recognized her own limits and began to teach her members about the nature of the church. We are, after all, intended to be a "priesthood of all believers"—to minister to one another. It is the responsibility of everyone!

[Nancy]

Yup. Though I wasn't in any of your congregations, I am one of those people you helped shepherd into ordained ministry. I remember carrying the fat, blue ring-binder into your office for six weeks of the Exploring Candidacy process. You kept all our appointments, read my papers, listened to my responses, and encouraged me to continue the process toward ordained ministry.

I valued your authority, but I didn't value your administrative expertise until my first year in the parish and the pastor's job was to submit January stats. I didn't have a clue on how to fill in hundreds of blanks. I called you. Loaded down with files, I met you in Green Bay at Zimmani's restaurant. I tasted a Smoky "Z" sandwich for the first time. And for the first time, I experienced your appetite for fun. After eating and digesting info on statistics, we found a pinball machine and used up all our quarters.

You won.

Avoid Murder and Lying
1 John 3.11–18
First UMC, Appleton (4/30/1989)

[Charlie]

... The first step is to know what love really is. We toss that word around, often without knowing that it means deep concern and caring; it means being aware of people and really making the attempt to see life through their eyes. Love means giving of one's self for others.

... When we love; when we get involved in another's life; when we risk a part of ourselves to establish a relationship; when we know a person on an individual basis and begin to see them the way God does—our attitudes and responses begin to change.

But some people are doggone difficult to love, aren't they? We just wish that God would change them and make them more easy to like and love. Or if God won't, then we'll work at it and try to change them ourselves—our spouse, our kids, our friends, an annoying church member. But when we examine the scriptures, we discover that Jesus said we are to love people just as they are. And if we find that too difficult, we can ask God to change *us* so that we can love them.

As one of the songs I used to sing at church camp put it, "Lord, make me more loving." It didn't say anything about changing others so they would be easier to love.

[Nancy]

Wait a minute, Charles. The title of your sermon was Avoid Murder and Lying. Except for a couple of paragraphs, you *avoided* those dark subjects and preached almost seven pages double-spaced on love. I know love is the topic of the entire book of 1 John, but ... well ... what about getting into the lives of people who lie and betray?

We both had spouses we'd promised to love forever. What happened? At 18, I just wanted to get out of my house. I really thought I loved him. Then I thought if I finished school, got a job, designed a passive solar home, I'd be satisfied. Happy even. I finished school. Got a job. Designed a passive solar home. Then looked down at my spouse from the loft in our new home. He wanted a new stereo, a motorcycle, another boat, a computer. I wanted a friend. I wasn't satisfied and certainly not happy. When did I realize I was the one who had to change?

Charlie, two months after you preached this sermon, we went to your thirty-fifth class reunion and announced our engagement. A year later we were married. I was happy—more than happy. At 50 years old, I was finally in love.

Some Dos and Don'ts When Suffering Comes (1)
Portions of Job; John 9.1–3a
First UMC, Appleton (8/24/1986)

[Charlie]
... The tragic thing about suffering, however, lies in the fact that when it falls upon us we appear to be so vulnerable and helpless. We cannot escape, it seems.

... No, we cannot! But we can come to some understanding about our world, ourselves, and our God that can help us escape some of the false ideas, the crippling attitudes and guilt surrounding pain—and the suffering and grief which follow. That's what I hope will happen today and then next

Sunday, since it will take at least two weeks to deal with this important issue.

... Three dos and don'ts when suffering comes:

1. Don't ever hesitate to ask questions, but do realize even as you ask, that we will never have all the answers.

2. Don't blame God, but do understand that God permits, allows, certain events.

3. Don't view all pain and suffering as sent by God as a punishment for sin. Do see that a good deal of it we bring on ourselves or else are victimized by the freedom given to others.

Some Dos and Don'ts When Suffering Comes (2)
Romans 8.28–39
First UMC, Appleton (8/31/1986)

[Charlie]
Often, just a few days after I've preached a sermon, I'll read a magazine article or book that concerned the same theme or text. And I'll regret that it hadn't arrived earlier. That would have happened this past week except that last Sunday's one sermon has turned into a three-part message. Thus, I can share with you this paragraph from an article in September's *Christian Ministry* magazine:

> Congregations and pastors who undertake a direct and thoughtful response to suffering ... should heed this caution: zeal to 'deal with' suffering ... should not override continuing pastoral sensitivity to the subject's threatening nature.

And the author, a hospital chaplain, goes on to note that efforts to correct "mistaken" beliefs about God and suffering should consider the importance that those beliefs may hold for particular people. He says, "It's inappropriate to wield 'theological broadaxes' to clear them away."

Well, I hope that my three "dos and don'ts" last Sunday didn't come across in that way.

... And now the fourth set of dos and don'ts: *Don't* be a fatalist and adopt the hopeless attitude of resignation which says, "What can I do about it?" or worse, "Whatever will be will be." But *do* understand the *law* of cause and effect.

The fifth set: *Don't* be overcome with evil. *Do* fight it, seeing this as an opportunity for personal growth.

The sixth set of dos and don'ts is this: When suffering comes, *don't* abandon God

(Does the pleading in my voice come through?) ... *Don't* abandon God! *Do* have confidence that God works for good with those who love God.

There's one more don't and do, but we're running out of time, so I'll add it to the things I planned to say next Sunday.

Some Dos and Don'ts When Suffering Comes (3)
Matthew 11.2–6; 2 Corinthians 1.3–7
First UMC, Appleton (9/7/1986)

[Charlie]

... I'm not going to review the first six dos and don'ts this morning. The last two sermons and this one have been printed and will be available for you to take home with you at the close of today's service. So for now let's move on to number seven: When suffering comes, *don't* hibernate; don't isolate yourself. *Do* seek out others for support. In fact, I would be more specific: Seek out others within the Christian community.

... When I taught the course "Suffering and the Christian Community of Faith" in Minnesota this past July, I gave out a crisis survey form. 325 responses from the people there were received; they indicated, as I suspected, that all of us have gone through suffering of one kind or another, but in the midst of the pain we often don't recognize that *we are not alone*. There is a Christian Community there to help. For example, 232 of the people indicated they had experienced emotional and verbal abuse by their spouse; nearly 9% were victims of sexual abuse when a child; 14% had lost a spouse through death; 15% were divorced; over 50% were acquainted with alcohol abuse themselves or experienced it through a family member or close friend. Over 4% had been raped; 12% had experienced loss of a body organ. And so it went through twenty-two different situations of pain and hurt.

... I really don't want to suffer, but I have and I will. I don't want to grieve, but I have and I will. I don't really want to die, but know that I will. Suffering and grief and death are part of life, and the decision to walk within and among every event as victor and not victim is a possibility given to every human being. Every event holds within it the possibility of new life, of new understanding, of new decisions to take hold and to live.

... God's help. that's the emphasis I want to bring forth out of so much that could still be said on this subject.

[Nancy]
Charlie, I read and reread these sermons, all of them printed and copied for church members. Over these three weeks you list seven dos and don'ts. The suggestions for each pairing are carefully and caringly explicated with quotes and stories. But the statements are either/or statements, as if one can separate dos and don'ts in the midst of abject suffering and pain.

I don't remember the days immediately following your death. I have journal scribblings during the three years of your increasing dementia. Some pages in red letters. Some just a written arrgh! But now? I remember being told by a nurse my fifteen minutes with your dead body was up. I remember a woman who stood in the hallway outside your room, another woman who greeted me at the door and walked with me to a table on the patio outside the building. She waited with me while I called your son.

I don't remember crying, like I just did. But the rest of that day? I must have driven home. I must have called the other children. I must have called the funeral home. But I don't remember all the names of people who called me, or people who came to our home.

And, God? You seem to be describing a supernatural god, a transcendent god outside of the suffering one, not a presence within, or immanent. I got A's on my theology papers, but it wasn't my ideas about God that helped me as I folded over in grief at your death. It was the grace-filled love of friends who called, emailed, sent cards, and showed up at our door with soup and flowers. And listened.

Just listened.

Charlie, these three sermons may help people who are helping *other* people in grief, but helping me cope in those first few days after your death? I couldn't have even read them.

Forget the Funeral
Mark 16.1–8
First UMC, Kenosha (4/3/1994)

[Charlie]

Sometimes I have trouble coming up with a sermon title. Other times I think of many possibilities. This was a day for which a number of titles came to me: "Unfinished Easter;" "If;" "Easter Exercise;" "Resurrection Reality." There was even an Easter title that could be someone's vanity license plate: "I GO B4U." But I concluded that the title "Forget the Funeral" was most appropriate today. You see, it speaks to those here who feel dead inside; who lack hope and power. And it describes the situation the disciples faced.

[Nancy]

Until this sermon, I thought I was done crying. Not the soft clear tears that slip down my cheeks every now and then, but the racking sobs. The title of this sermon got me. There was no funeral to forget. Because of Covid, you were remembered for about five minutes during an October Sunday morning worship service held out on the church lawn. People sat in folding chairs six feet apart. We sang #707, one of your favorites.

In the bulb there is a flower, in the seed, an apple tree ...
... in our end is our beginning, in our time, infinity ...

You had been dead a month.

As I read the sermon with soggy tissue, I wondered how bound-up grief becomes so quickly untethered by a simple memory. What else had I forgotten in those first few weeks after your death? I opened the drawer with my various journals, emails, and papers and found the polka-dotted notebook we bought years earlier when we heard your diagnosis. We planned to write things I would need to know if and when you became incapacitated, but because we only managed to record one thing (hot tub maintenance) a few months before your death I began using the notebook as a journal.

Here's what I wrote the day after you died:

>Sept.11, 2020
>#182 Covid day
>
>After
>I kissed his forehead
>put his wedding ring back
>on his finger still warm
>said goodbye
>and began drive home
>two sandhill cranes
>flew in front of windshield
>two
>and two trees
>limbs fresh cut leaning
>over our driveway
>two
>this morning only one sun pushed through
>steel skin of the throbbing lake
>one
>shown gold
>across shimmering waves to me
>before being swallowed
>by clouds.

What Do You Mean, Salvation?
Romans 5.1–11
LaPaz Community Church (4/30/1967)

[Charlie]
"What do you really mean when you speak of salvation?" someone asked me last year. It seemed to me that a lot of people have this question in their minds and that an attempt to answer it should be made in a sermon. Here is a word that is used a lot, but with many meanings for some; one definite ever unchangeable meaning for others, and little or no significance for the rest, other than a vague feeling that here is something profound and holy. Let us right now admit that the average man today who doesn't attend church couldn't care less about salvation. And many who do attend aren't sure why they should care either.

A cartoon in a college newspaper shows a spacecraft on a desolate planet. The man who has descended from the craft carries a Bible in his hand, and his space suit has a clerical collar. He is surrounded by little green men, one of whom is asking, "You have come here to save us from what?"

... What then do we mean by salvation? "Happy certainty" as Phillips translates Paul's words: ... the primary emphasis is on the attitude of confidence rather than upon physical circumstances. It means that one will be free from any fear of the unknown, the unknown of today, the unknown of twenty or fifty years from now. Though difficulties of all sorts are certain to come, and death very definitely will approach, the "saved" Christian will rest secure in the knowledge that he is under God's care and always will be.

[Nancy]

Oh Charlie. I don't know where to start. The preceding sermon "Forget the Funeral" undid me. Distressed I fell backward into—and got stuck replaying—those last four months of your life. In conversation with Dwight, my spirit guide, I decided to take a month's break from this writing.

On Friday, July 1, (2022). I lit the candle, rang the bell, and read the Tagore poem, the same brief writing I used the day your kids sifted your ashes into Lake Michigan. During the month I did some other reading and writing, met with friends, and facilitated some classes at North Pointe. On July 30, your birth date and the first anniversary of your interment, I walked the sunlit path to the Lake and watched the gentle turquoise waves kiss the steps. You would have been 86 years old.

I met with Dwight on August 1. He was silent while I lit the candle, rang the bell, and read Tagore. Then I opened the drawer with the remaining pile of your sermons and this sermon was on the top. *What Do You Mean, Salvation?* Yuck! Immediately I heard "Are you saved?" the familiar question coming as a warning about where I will end up after death if I haven't experienced the right holy thing or said the right Jesus words.

Charlie, months ago, when I first came across this sermon, I read the above two opening paragraphs and almost threw it out. The very word *salvation* is distasteful. I only *saved* this sermon because it was preached in Bolivia and you were only 30 years old.

Then last Sunday I began facilitating a six-week class which follows the soul journey of John Wesley. As we watch the videos about this founder of Methodism, we're exploring our own faith unfolding and all those old terms are coming up: Sin, Grace, Salvation.

Was it a coincidence that this sermon was on the top of this unfinished conversation with you? Now I've read this sermon in its entirety and you used features of scripture, theology, psychology, and that little green men cartoon to transform the old meaning of salvation into terms that I understand and believe in. I don't know when or where, but I am aware of an internal confidence that I can draw on in the face of fear. Well, if, in the midst of a paralyzed terror, I remember its presence.

Thank you.

Here's the Tagore poem.

> *Let it not be death, but completeness.*
> *Let love melt into memory and pain into songs.*
> *Let the flight through the sky end in the wings folding over the nest.*
> *Let the last touch of your hands be gentle like the flower of the night.*
> *Stand still, O Beautiful End, for a moment and say your last words in silence.*
> *We bow to you and hold up our lamps to light you on your way.*
>
> ~ Rabindranath Tagore

Christian Perfection
Philippians 3.10–16; Matthew 5.43–48
First UMC, Kenosha (7/18/1993)

[Charlie]

Deep down in the inner pocket of a suit coat I found this slip of paper one day. It says,

Examiner No. 21. To our customers: This garment was carefully examined and should be perfect.

Wow! It didn't just pass or get an okay; it's perfect! Wouldn't it be great if human beings could pass such an inspection? The first three panels of this cartoon make it seem possible: A man says, "I haven't said a harsh word to anyone in days. I haven't misused my friends or spoken ill of my neighbor. Maybe I'm cultivating some Christian graces." Then in the fourth picture we see that he is standing alone on a small island, and he concludes: "Still, I'd sure like to get back to civilization."

Professor Claude Thompson took a study leave from his theological school. While reading in a library someone asked him what he was doing. "I'm studying the Methodist doctrine of Christian perfection," he replied. "Well," said the other, "I don't believe in the perfection of anybody, especially the Methodists."

These two illustrations each contain an important fact about Christian perfection: first, that it has to do with relationships—perfection and isolation just don't go together; second, Methodism indeed has been associated with the concept of perfection. In fact, John Wesley believed God raised up the people called Methodists to proclaim the truth of Christian perfection.

[Nancy]

Ah. Perfection. Another old word I have had to integrate. Again, I only kept this sermon because you had the faded and wrinkled green slip of paper you found in your pocket fastened to the front page with one of your rusty paper clips, obviously, one of the clips you saved from our basement flood.

I have two immediate responses to your sermon. First, yesterday's class at North Pointe UMC listed "religious" words we've been saddled with (sin, grace, salvation, conversion, conviction, redemption, etc.) and, second, years ago I learned that the word *perfect* in the Bible was translated from a Greek word *telos* which means fulfilled purpose.

Regarding my life, I have no idea what my purpose is or has been, let alone know if I'm fulfilling it. I think of the title of a Dylan Thomas poem: *The force that through the green fuse shoots the flower.* Do I block that force? Am I still trying to bloom? Maybe I've already bloomed and now my petals are falling, the stem is drooping.

I think *perfection* is a process and knowing I'm loved coaxes the flower along into blooming. You were the one who most nurtured my growing.

Frederick Buechner died last week. Yesterday, I took his book *Whistling in the Dark* to class. After another hour of unpacking old words that have fed our guilt for so many centuries, I read a few of Buechner's words:

> ... the Truth that Christianity claims to be true is ultimately to be found, if it's to be found at all, not in the Bible, or the Church, or Theology—the best they can do is point to the Truth—but in our own stories.

Charlie, I believe you found that "examiner's slip of perfection" in the dark blue suit you bought to wear at our wedding. I don't know if my image is true, but I'm putting it in my story.

What is the Spiritual LIfe?
*1 Corinthians 3.1–3, 16–17; 1 Peter2.1–5;
Colossians 3.12–17
First UMC, Kenosha (8/16/1992)*

[Charlie]

Earlier in my ministry one of the criticisms I heard about myself was that I was not spiritual enough. Now as one who takes criticism perhaps too much to heart, I tried to understand what was meant by that; but when I questioned my critics I always got vague responses. Spirituality is something sensed or felt, they said, "and we just don't believe that you have enough of it."

... Well, my examination led inward. And though I *knew* that the peace of Christ ruled in my heart, I knew also that I didn't pray as well as either the saints or even some other pastors I knew; the time I set aside for morning prayer and devotions often got interrupted or squeezed by other demands upon my time; holy phrases and Scripture passages seldom came out of my mouth; I didn't keep a journal or meditate much; I was not one to share a lot of my inner life and struggles with others; and I was young—and even younger looking than my actual age.

Except for the fact that now I'm neither young or young-looking, little else has changed in that list of things that I thought made one spiritual; but somewhere along the way the criticisms of the 1970s ceased. Perhaps because of a lot of *other* changes in my life. However, my feelings of guilt and inadequacy about my spiritual life and practices did not die off.

And so early in the 1980s, when the term "Spiritual Formation" began to circulate in church circles, all these feelings of mine were reinforced. Spirituality was "in" and there were retreats, academies, seminary courses, video tapes and a multitude of books to guide pilgrims along the spiritual path. So, I attended retreats and bought lots of books and cassette tapes, and tried various disciplines—imaging, meditation, contemplating icons, molding clay, body movement. Now I consider it time well spent. Still, I felt guilty because most of that which I attempted seemed more a chore than a joy and I didn't sustain any of these activities for long.

Then one day my wife, a few months before she became my wife, told me that I probably was a more spiritual person than she. That really stunned me! This from a person who has a prayer bench in her room, and who journals regularly and who *enjoys* spiritual retreats and who can meditate and not be bored!

Then, not long ago, I acquired and read a book by Parker Palmer. He sounded like me—guilty because he just wasn't able to find much satisfaction and fulfillment in the spiritual disciplines and other activities that some of his friends advocated. And oh, how he had tried!

Now my wife had *attempted* to explain to me what she meant by calling me spiritual. She felt that in my daily living, my reactions, my enthusiasm and love of life and ministry I was in the presence of God, living within the Kingdom, already experiencing what others were trying to find. Her explanations were helpful, but it took Parker Palmer, PhD, theologian, professor and author (and a male, my wife points out) to move me along further in my thinking. "For me," he said, "the heart of the spiritual quest is to know 'the rapture of being alive,' and to allow that knowledge to transform us into celebrants, advocates, defenders of a life wherever we find it. For some of us, the primary path to that aliveness is called the active life."

And to that I said, "Yes!"

[Nancy]

Charlie, I smiled throughout reading this. You preached this thirty years ago. From my experience with you, except for the last four months of your life, you lived every one of those days with enthusiasm, curiosity, and generosity.

I still slog through my days. In addition to calling the plumber, paying the bills, and answering emails, I meditate, journal, write, and fiddle around with art supplies. (Oh yes. that seiza bench belonged to my psychiatrist. I still don't know how I ended up with it or where it is now.) Once in a while I'll read an article, visit with a friend, try a new recipe, and find myself even enthused. Temporarily. But knowing the 'rapture of being alive?' Not so much.

Frankly, some of your incessant, bubbly, enthusiasm pissed me off.

However, I am in touch with something within me that is constantly present and provides some assurance, especially when things go awry, but I don't have a name for it.

I don't know what being "spiritual" means either, but I'm for all those books you bought and workshops you attended. At least you knew what I was talking about.

Joseph and That Coat
Genesis 37 (selected)
Wauwatosa Avenue UMC (8/7/2011)

[Charlie]

... I've never repeated a sermon that I preached previously in another church, but I certainly go back to get ideas and illustrations from old sermons. And when I looked up

Joseph, I discovered that it was in June, 1997, 14 years ago, that I had preached about Joseph. And rereading my words *then* was as painful *now* as it was *then*.

Here's part of what I told the folks in Kenosha: "This has been a tough weekend for me. I have no brothers, only one sister, and she has three sons. This weekend the oldest of the boys is being married in the bride's hometown of DePere. I wasn't invited to the wedding because my sister cut off all contact with me eight years ago. Two of my three children weren't invited to their cousin's wedding because I learned my sister said, 'They are too much like their father ... they remind me of my brother.'"

I continue to write to her, but get no response. And the sad thing is that I have never ever been told what it is that so angered her and created the separation. I would welcome the opportunity to ask her forgiveness for whatever it may be that led to her bitterness. And as I thought about this, I knew I wasn't alone. Many of you have experienced similar situations.

The comments I received (then) and the persons wanting to talk to me about their own painful situations following those words indicated the degree of hurt people are living with.

[Nancy]

Charlie, though you explore the behaviors of Joseph and his brothers and preach wisely about relationships, forgiveness, and reconciliation, I'm not going to respond to the other five and a half pages of this sermon. Rather I want to comment on the estrangement between you and your sister that troubled you throughout our marriage. Though your ex-wife and children knew the cause of the rift, they would not share it with you—or me, either. The shunning hurt you. Furthermore, not knowing what you had done prevented you from forgiving yourself.

You heard about your sister's death from your son. According to his contact with your nephews, you were to stay away from the funeral. Though you were dealing with dementia, the fresh rejection brought new tears. We sent a donation to a Women's Resource Center that was named in her obituary.

Charlie, in this sermon about Joseph, you also spoke of change. As I've read through the boxes of your sermons, I've seen evidence of a gradual change in you. Judgmentalism into compassion. Obsession with work into play. And personal hurts into healing.

Your sister's decision meant years of aching loss that could have been rich with loving family connections. So sad.

How to Know Right From Wrong
1 Peter 1.13–16
Trinity UMC, Racine (9/22/1974)

[Charlie]
... Now having said all this, let's talk about how we can figure out what to do when decisions must be made. And I have no four steps for you to follow in order—one, two, three, four—and you'll never have any more problems. Instead, I have four sound principles, all of which must be used and tested against one another in order that the correct course of action will more likely come forth.

... First of all, the Christian has access to the Bible and should use it ...

... use the lessons of the past to gain insight and strength. One Christian teacher strongly suggests that all of us need to put aside some of the novels and trash that we read and take up reading biographies: learn how men and women of faith sought to obey God in those life situations in which He placed them ...

...A third source to consider in decision-making is the Holy Spirit, the inner voice.

...A fourth principle is always to act from the motive of love. We should all be "Who-askers"—who will be helped or hurt, and not "What-askers"—what does the law demand?

[Nancy]

Charlie, I saved this sermon and the following two, all preached in the 1970s as examples of your moralizing early in your ministry. Though in this sermon you acknowledge the complicated world folks lived in and the struggle to make good decisions, you give no examples of tough situations folks may have faced. You spend the first three pages describing how we get tripped up trying to figure out right and wrong. When you finally get to the four principles—on page four—they are all *shoulds* and we *musts*.

Then you end with,

"As our Scripture said today: 'Therefore, as obedient children, do not let your character be shaped any longer by the desires you cherished in your days of ignorance. The One who called you is holy; like him, be holy in all your behavior.'"

What?! What's with the underlined "your" behavior? Are you implying all *your* decisions are *right*? Are you "Who-asking" who will be helped or hurt by your words? I don't know how your church members heard this in 1974, but I would have left worship that day feeling definitely inadequate and terribly guilty.

This stuff gives me the hives.

Playing at Religion
Luke 7.24–35
Trinity UMC, Racine (10/27/1974)

[Charlie]

I was living in Bolivia when a new adult game came out, but I read all about it in *Newsweek*.

It was called "Merit," and was played somewhat like Monopoly. All players receive baptismal cards and a stack of merit slips. Counters are plastic statues of Jesus, Mary, Joseph, and an angel. You move your statue around the board by answering correctly questions about the beliefs and practices of the Roman Catholic church. During the game each player is required to help build a church, convent, seminary, and several other buildings. The outside of the box urges adults to buy the game by quoting from Matthew's Gospel: "Unless you become as little children, you shall not enter the Kingdom."

What a wrenching of Matthew's words from their context! And what a disgusting game! In fact, some of the questions and the answers you are supposed to give are downright obscene from a truly Christian point of view. But to me the whole thing points up the fact that a lot of people treat their religion as a game; they play at it, don't take it very seriously, and drop out from the game whenever they take a mind to. The parable I read for our lesson today was spoken by Jesus to give us an example of the way people play at their religion.

[Nancy]

Oh my. I read the scripture from Luke. It is not a parable, Charlie. It's a red-letter rant attributed to Jesus. You obviously took your "master's" cue. This is another example of your early tendency to scold. You rail for six pages about the ways folks avoid the serious challenges of being Christian. I kept hoping you would put Matthew's words about being a child in context. You know, wonder and play. But there is no such softening evident in your scolds. And, you haven't caught on to inclusive gender pronouns for the Holy One. Yet.

Your ending? A scorching tirade: "So enough of this playing at being a Christian and trying to dictate the rules of the game! God, in his patience, invites us *now* to follow the Way of his son. Stop playing around!"

In 1982, shortly after we met and I began my six-week "Candidate for Ministry" process with you, another pastor said, "Charlie's a straight arrow. He'll be a big help to you in your process, but you wouldn't want to spend an evening with him."

The Handwriting on the Wall
Daniel 5 (selected verses)
Oconomowoc UMC (5/15/77)

[Charlie]
... *Christian Century* writer, James Wall, says that "A sermon is a means whereby one member of the Christian community shares with others his vision of the relevancy of the Biblical tradition at the present moment ..." That's exactly what I've tried to do this morning. The handwriting is on the wall for us. Can you read it? It's there for you and me and not just for the Babylonians and Belshazzar; it's not there just for the Greeks and their cruel king. It's a message for those of us who trust solely in the things of this life and thus are idolators; for those of us who mock the good things of this creation and blaspheme God with our words and actions; it's a message for

those of us who refuse or don't take the trouble to learn from the past, thinking in our pride that we can find all the answers on our own, and then wonder why we fail; it's a word for all who hear the words of judgment spoken, but go on thinking that "it won't touch my life, it won't happen in my generation, he's not talking about me."

Read and understand the writing on the wall!

[Nancy]

Geez. I don't know why I saved these last three dreadful examples of your moralizing. For some reason, finding proof of your judgmentalism initially pleased me. Here was affirmation of the "straight arrow" rep you once had. But quickly following was a feeling of gratitude for whom you *became*.

Of course, you were still in your 30s when you spouted this dogma. How would I have responded to your pontificating if you had been my pastor then? Actually, I had the similar right and wrong indoctrination from my parents and the church. Not only was I uncomfortable with it then, but the scolding rules left me emotionally bereft, longing to feel loved in spite of my inevitable "bad" behavior.

Interestingly enough, Charlie, we both have strong morality police patrolling our actions. Was it our love and trust for each other that kept them restrained?

Do you remember the night I came home from another church meeting where I had to respond to the group that had formed to get rid of me? I came into the family room. You were in the hot tub, saw me enter, raised your eyebrows in an unspoken, "Well, how did it go?"

"God damn it!" I hollered and sailed my folder across the room, papers scattering and floating onto the carpet.

I can still see your face, rosy pink from 102-degree water, blanch white at my blasphemy. But you didn't say a word. Rather, you swallowed, got out of the comforting water and into the rough waves of my distress.

What would you say about these sermons now, Charlie? Would you defend yourself? Be embarrassed? Would you try to talk me out of printing them? I hope not. I want to include these because I don't want to "betray" you in some way by making you sound like a saint. More importantly, they reveal a great contrast to your later sermons which attest to your gradual growth in compassion.

Something I'm still working on.

You Can't Keep A Secret
Colossians 1.24–29
First UMC, Appleton (7/27/1986)

[Charlie]

I remember some advice I was given by my senior pastor while I was a seminary student and serving as his assistant in West Allis. He said that in summertime we should preach "lighter" sermons—by that he meant to go easy on heavy theology; don't choose subjects that engage the minds of the people in the congregations to any great extent; don't wrestle with great issues or raise disturbing question in the summer.

I'm deeply indebted to that pastor for so much in my ministry, but that suggestion about lightening up summer sermons was one thing I chose to ignore. In fact, the lectionary readings—Scripture selected to be read in many denominations each Sunday—certainly engages the mind in summer. We've been looking at Paul's letters to the churches in Galatia and Colossae. In them the apostle raises important issues of faith.

... While I'm no longer frightened of bishops and district superintendents, I still hold all of them in awe and a great deal of respect. Therefore, when I was speaking at the Minnesota School of Christian Mission a couple of weeks ago and learned two days into the class that there were two district superintendents in the group of two hundred, I gulped a bit. But then the neatest thing happened—one of those men sought me out and thanked me for the way I had started the class. You see, I had shared something of myself and my own struggles and discoveries in the midst of suffering. He then related how a Pastor-Parish Relations Committee in the church he served before going on the district urged him to tell more of his own life story, particularly his personal struggles in the Christian life. And we talked, then, about how this went contrary to the way we had been taught to preach in seminary many years before, and how we have both changed a bit and yet how difficult it is to be vulnerable and say, "I don't know," or "I'm hurting, too," or "I'm struggling," or "Here's my story."

... The secret, the mystery is simply this: Christ is in you and me.

... To proclaim Christ, to teach the secret of Christ in us to others, doesn't mean we have to talk about the past or our success in living as a Christian. ... It just means to be open and able to say, "Here are some areas I'm struggling with, and here's how I see the Christ guiding me through." Let's try to think of witnessing more along those lines—telling our story.

[Nancy]

What happened to you, Charlie, that you began sharing your own "rough edges?" In the early 1980s, while I was an Inquiring Candidate and then a Field Ed student at First UMC in Appleton, you shared some of your family problems. And as part of my process toward ordination, I needed to be honest about my relationship with my then husband.

In those days our conversations included theological ideas, church work, and personal issues. But Christ in me? The *word* "Christ" trips me up. I don't have a word for "something" within me I was unaware of until my psychotic break. During that break, I got in touch with "something" with me and within me that I've learned to trust, especially in the midst of humiliation, stigma, and shunning. I can't call it "Christ," or "Master" or "Jesus" or whatever else you called it, but I know our trust in "something" was present in our early conversations.

Barbara Ehrenreich died a few days ago. When asked in an interview about a mystical experience, she said "there is a realm that transcends words." I like that phrase. And I treasure the times we spent together in that mystical space.

The Borrowing Christ
Matthew 5.42
First UMC, Kenosha (6/18/2000)

[Charlie]

I had been pastor here for three or four years when, one Sunday morning while the choir was singing, I looked over at those two large metal plates on the west well of the sanctuary. "I wonder what you have to do in order to get a big plaque like that?" I asked myself. And then reality struck. Both of those pastors named on the plates died while they were serving this church. "Never mind," I thought. "If that's what it takes, I never want my name on a plaque over there" And now I think I'm in the clear—just a few more minutes!

It was November 16, 1952 at the Mt. Washington Methodist Church in Cincinnati, Ohio when I preached my first sermon. I was just sixteen-years old and a junior in high school. Today I want to tell you about that message; in fact, I'll be sharing a part of that sermon with you ...

Before I get to that first sermon which is included in this last sermon, I want to mention some other matters. I'm wearing my first clerical robe. It was a gift from my parents upon my ordination in 1959. It served me well for many years, but began to wear out about the time that other lighter colors started to replace black—colors which communicated worship as a celebration. My stole today is one of several I have which came from Bolivia—a place I lived and served in for 5½ years and which helped shape who I am today.

Here are some statistics—of interest perhaps only to me (but since I did the research, I'm going to pass them on to you anyway): During my ministry I've conducted 317 funerals, 196 weddings, and I have preached 1,440 sermons. Now some of those sermons were preached two, three, and four times a weekend. I calculated, therefore, that I have preached for 1,018 hours—assuming the sermons were 22 minutes in length. Of course, some were a bit longer than that, weren't they?

... Over the years of my ministry there have been lots of comments concerning my energy and my enthusiasm. The energy just must be genetic, I suppose, but the enthusiasm comes in large part, I'm convinced, from my call to the ordained ministry and the assurance I have received over the years that this was indeed what God intended for my life. The pains, troubles, conflicts, meetings, and misunderstandings that go with being a pastor have had an effect on my life, certainly, but they have been overcome as I have received the gift of joy at being called into Christ's service—a call that has been affirmed over and over.

And that statement takes me back to 1952 and that very first sermon called "The Borrowing Christ." The text was from Matthew 5.42: "Give to everyone who begs from you, and do not refuse anyone who wants to borrow from you."

Now I pulled that one verse completely out of context, using it in a way that I later learned one should not do in preaching. But what did I know?

Well, here goes: ...

[Nancy]

Charlie. How were you to know that you would preach "The Borrowing Christ" *one more time* before you *finally* retired? Reading through boxes you left of your sermons, I found three in which you spoke about your call: your original one, which is missing; this one—your "official" retirement sermon; and the one you preached at Wauwatosa, twelve years after you had retired. Actually, with all our interims, you retired seven times.

I love that you included stats. You kept incredible records. And, you counted. Steps to the mailbox. Miles to the Kenosha church. Minutes from home to I-94. Your notebook keeping track of our finances overwhelmed me.

But the story of your call? 1952. If you were alive, what would you want included? Before you turn to your own "call" story, you name fifteen people as examples of individuals from whom God "borrowed." When you finally get to the story of Christ "borrowing" you, the telling is almost identical to the later account.

This paragraph is repeated word for word:

On Thursday night, or to be more accurate, Friday morning, I could not sleep. Well, Reverend Taylor and I talked together for about two hours while we were lying in our bunks. After my conversation with Reverend Taylor and the Friday night Consecration Service, I attended the Saturday morning communion service and turned in my commitment card for Christ—to give my life to Christ as minister.

Oh Sweetheart. The first time you shared this pivotal story with me, I got angry. Not at you, but the still simmering memory of my 1953 summer camp. You told parts of your call story in other sermons. I've told my summer camp story many times as well.

A surprise for me this time, as I reflected on your story, is the similarity in our formative one-week church camp events: Consecration night, inspiring sermons, candles, commitment. Yours 1952. Mine 1953. Though your commitment was clear and supported, mine was confusing and restricted. You've heard this story many times: "You may be wondering what this means," the pastor crooned to those of us who went "all the way" with Jesus in our commitment. "Boys, you could become ministers. Girls, you could become minister's wives."

Five years later, at 18, I went "all the way" into a 29-year marriage with a future high school principal and only gradually began to realize my limited social power due to my gender.

Now 2022. Somewhere during all those ensuing years, I became both a pastor and a pastor's wife. When I asked you to marry me, did you remember Jesus' call "not to refuse anyone who wants to borrow from you?"

What is a Christian?
Matthew 4.18–22
Wauwatosa Avenue UMC (1/26/2014)

[Charlie]

This happened about thirty-five years ago, but I remember it so clearly. I was pastor in Oconomowoc and drove in to Elm Grove to act in plays at the Sunset Playhouse. On one occasion I was at a cast party at someone's home when a young woman who was also in the play came over to me and asked, "You're a minister, right?" I told her that yes I was. "Well, I want to know what Christianity is all about. I don't know anything about it." She'd never been in a church, never read a Bible, and the subject had never ever come up in her home.

Last year I was on a tour of countries in Eastern Europe, our leader was a young man from Hungary. One day he sat down next to me on the bus and asked if I were a priest. I told him no, but I was a Protestant minister—a United Methodist pastor. And for the next hour and a half we talked religion. He had many, many questions. Now we had visited several shrines and churches, yet he had little understanding of Christianity. I thought I was speaking softly, but I learned later that our voices were reaching the twenty-six other people on the bus.

Just what is a Christian? How would *you* explain it? Today's Scripture offers some insight.

Consider this: As Jesus walked along the shore of the Sea of Galilee there was not a Christian in the whole world. Peter, Andrew, James, and John were probably good people who tried to keep the laws of their Hebrew faith, but they weren't Christians—until and when they responded to Jesus' invitations: "Follow me." "Come with me." "Join me." A Christian therefore, is someone who responds to the call of Jesus. We are Christians because of Someone. A scholar notes that the word "Christian" means literally, "Partisan of Christ," a member of Christ's party. The word implies a commitment of life, a decision, a choice. It is very clear what side a partisan is on. And Christians are so because of their relationship to Jesus.

[Nancy]

"Partisan of Christ!" Charlie! What were you reading? Had you already found the academic work of the Westar Christianity Seminar? If so, why didn't you tell me? Of course, the book I'm excited about now wasn't printed until last year, but the scholarly work has been going on since the Nag Hammadi Library was translated. I want someone to talk with who really cares about this stuff.

And, *partisan*! Recent evidence suggests the word "Christian" wasn't even used until a couple hundred years after Jesus was dead.

Well, Charlie, if there is an afterlife and if you are present with me in some form now, or maybe given a pass to some library in the sky where my writing shows up, you will know that with my new understanding, I'm buying books, babbling to friends, and browsing the website trying to deal with my Christian label.

Of course, I was baptized. And because Mother saved everything, I have the old certificate (June 16, 1940) as well as the marked paid hospital bill for my birth. ($55.25 for nine days) Obviously, I didn't have a choice about being branded Christian. When I *did* have a choice, at Confirmation, I just wanted to wear stockings and heels for the first time. Never mind the garters cut into my legs and I couldn't keep the seams on the nylons straight. I had no clue to what I was promising. Two months later, I went to the unforgettable summer church camp and committed my life to Jesus.

Marriage, four children, commitment to St. Elizabeth's, the seminary thing, divorce, you, and suddenly I found myself standing in front of people wearing a Holy Ghost outfit. Who knows how it happened?

Now? Forty years later I'm reading *The Gospel of Mary* and *After Jesus Before Christianity*. I don't sound like a "Partisan of Jesus." I don't sound like a partisan of anybody.

Making Human Relations Christian
Ephesians 4.22–24; 3.1–5.2; James 2.1, 8–9
First UMC, Kenosha   (1/17/1993)

[Charlie]
"On Being a Christian Outside the Church." This has been our theme during January. And this weekend is Human Relations weekend—in many churches and denominations throughout our land. Putting those things together, therefore, has led to today's subject: "Being a Christian in our Human Relationships"—particularly those relationships with people not like us: those of other colors, cultures, and countries. Yes, I'm going to talk about racism.

But I want to start with a warning which was prompted by a line from a poem: "Preconceived ideas are hardest to destroy: the roots go deeper ..."

I know *that's* true: now, add to that the fact that prejudice enhances some people's self-esteem; it meets certain psychological needs; and I'm left wondering just how much effect one sermon can have in leading us to start digging out our preconceived notions—or at least creating an awareness of them and a desire to do something about the situation.

Well, let's try; let's see what can be done in the time we have together today ...

... Now all the contacts, conversations, and reading we can engage in still will not bring us to the point where we can really identify with and understand the feelings, resentment, and bitterness of minorities. I can try to walk in their shoes, and see through their eyes but I certainly can never get into the skin of others. And I fight defensiveness in myself, too.

... Few of us have permitted ourselves really to *hear* the sounds, to *see* the brokeness, to experience frustrations and anger and passion and the utter defeat that the past has left in many. As one person said to the writer Studs Turkle: "I don't think most whites understand what it is to be black in the U.S. today. They don't even have a clue." But I believe it is so important that we try to hear and see, even if we cannot experience what it means.

As World War Two was drawing to a close, an elementary-age school girl in Cincinnati, Ohio won an essay contest centered on the theme: "What would be the most appropriate punishment for Adolph Hitler?" The thesis of this girl's essay was that the best punishment for Hitler would be to put him in a black skin and make him live the rest of his life in America. Wow! When I read about this girls' response a few years ago it became for me one of those moments of revelation. It struck me that I was the same age as that black girl, and I also grew up in the Cincinnati area. And I certainly wasn't aware that there were such serious problems or that the feelings ran that deep.

But then I began to remember things: Like my parents expressing their gratitude that Negroes weren't allowed into Coney Island, Cincinnati's amusement park. I learned that blacks could swim in the city pools only after the white kids had swum, then the pools were drained. I knew that many whites intentionally stayed away from Cincinnati's Crosley Field when the Brooklyn Dodgers and Jackie Robinson came to town to play the Reds, since the place "would be crowded with all those Negroes." We had just one black family in my suburban township school, but there was racism being expressed even in the way people talked about them: "The Jacksons are such a nice family." In other words, they are an exception.

I'm a 56-year-old white male who grew up in an all-white community outside Cincinnati and attended an all-white church and went to an all-white school—except for the Jackson kids—and I had parents who planted a lot of ideas in my head about Blacks, Roman Catholics, Jews, the Japanese, Hillbillies, Indians ... Much has been purged, but even I'm not really sure how much remains—until something happens and I react and classify people.

... Racism! I never heard the word as a kid. And a lot has changed, but I wonder what attitudes my grandchildren will point to as evidence of our continuing racism—things we are simply unable to see right now? The racism that is right here—much of it still unrecognized?

I have hope since many changes for good have already come about in our generation. Of course, I'm a White saying that, and Whites traditionally say, "Look how far you've come." Minorities reply: "Look how far we've got to go." And we are both right. But at least the ground is being broken up so we can continue to get at, expose, and tear out the old destructive ideas and sinister forces that lie deep-rooted below the surface.

So let us use the occasion of this Human Relations Weekend to ask the Lord to help us in continuing our task of the Christian work of reconciliation. And may the words of our Biblical Witness today challenge us: "Get rid of all bitterness and wrath and anger and wrangling and slander and malice. Instead, be kind and tender-hearted to one another, and forgive one another, as God in Christ has forgiven you."

[Nancy]

Oh my. Throughout your ministry you tackled the hard stuff. In this *thirty-year-old* seven-page double-spaced discourse, you define racism, give some history, acknowledge your "whiteness," share your experience as a child in Cincinnati, confess your sin, and build your comments on the Biblical injunction to "be kind to one another ... to live in love, as Christ loved us and gave himself up for us ..."

If you were still alive, I'd ask you if there was any response from folks who heard these words. Now, I wonder if any of those folks were watching two years ago while riots, triggered by racial tension, raged on the Kenosha streets in front of the church you served for eleven years.

Though you were alive during those late August, 2020 days, you weren't cognizant of the cultural upheaval since the death of a Black man at the hands of Minneapolis police. And, though I was aware of and sympathetic to the Black Lives Matter movement, I was preoccupied, stumbling through the wreckage of your dementia. May 25, the day George Floyd was suffocated, you were at Shorelight, kicking, and throwing coffee at the additional caretakers who had to be with you 24/7. And, two memory care facilities later, when Kenosha went up in a riot of flames, I was arranging to have you transferred by ambulance from the geriatric psych unit in Amita in Bolingbrook to Burr Oak, Genoa City, where you would die—alone—ten days later.

Oh Charlie. When I look at my scribblings during those last few weeks, of your life, the political erosion of trust, the world in a Covid-19 upheaval, and climate change, I can hardly believe folks keep picking up the pieces and trying to put broken lives and hearts back together.

And what has the United Methodist Church done in the past 30 years? After years of conversations, polity arguments, and protests, the church is splitting over LGBTQA+ issues. Thank some god or other that I'm connected with a United Methodist Community of Faith that has rainbow flags in its outdoor planters.

Praise the Lord
Psalm 147
Wauwatosa Avenue UMC (2/8/2015)

[Charlie]

Sometimes we pastors struggle a bit to find hymns that tie into the message of the day. That certainly wasn't a problem today. Every hymn I selected contains references to praising God. And then when I showed Nancy this Sunday's bulletin she expressed her disappointment that I hadn't selected hymn 109. Here's stanza one (of that hymn):

> *Creating God, your fingers trace*
> *the bold design of farthest space;*
> *let sun and moon and stars and light*
> *and what lies hidden praise your might.*

"Praise the Lord." Some folks use that phrase rather regularly and that's great! Others—me included—say those words more infrequently, but I have thought and said that phrase more frequently since mid-November. I'm grateful for hundreds or even thousands of scientists who have produced medicines and procedures which can cure my cancer, probably. I'm grateful for the six different physicians I have had contact with. I'm grateful for this church—for you—and your cards and notes telling of your support, understanding and prayers. The other day I found this quotation in my files. A character in Shakespeare's *Twelfth Night* says: "I hate ingratitude more in a person than lying, vainness, babbling drunkenness, or any taint of vice whose strong corruptions inhabits our frail blood."

Well, there is no ingratitude *here*!

Today's text is the 147th Psalm. ... These verses constitute a powerful and forceful statement of the greatness of God. When I first wrote those words down, instantly the first words of the prayer I was taught by my parents to say at dinner time came to mind: "God is great and God is good, and we thank God for our food..."

[Nancy]

Well, the prayer you said as a kid at mealtime is the same one my family said. Though you didn't include the rest of the blessing—*By his hand we all are fed. Thank you Lord for daily bread*—I still remember bowing my head and mumbling the words without being the least bit thankful for the slimy green beans.

When I first sorted the three boxes of your sermons, I almost threw this one out because of the title. These days "Praise the Lord" seems to be said most often by folks who give allegiance to a gun-totin' Jesus. I saved the sermon because your reference to cancer appeared on the first page and the date will help fasten my memories of your chemo and radiation treatments into a time and place.

This homily also made the second and third cuts because inserted into the bulletin were seven half-sheets with quotes you used as you preached. I wanted an example of your record keeping. Below each typed passage, you printed when and where you used the reference. According to your tiny penciled notations, you used the yellow-edged Shakespeare quote five times: Bolivia (11/23/66); Trinity (8/8/71); Oconomowoc (2/8/81); Appleton (2/8/84); and in this Wauwatosa sermon preached while you were dealing with cancer.

Charlie, I threw away hundreds and hundreds of half-sheets that represented hours and hours of your study and work. Most of the hundreds of cartoons you saved on half-sheets were also recycled. The two metal boxes which contained those sixty years worth of quotes and anecdotes you used for sermon illustrations have been donated to St. Vincent's.

I have promised myself I will finish this project of sermon conversations with you by Thanksgiving Day. The date may seem arbitrary, but as I read all five pages of your words about God's creative activity and goodness, my jaded opinions about The Holy One and Company melted into gratitude. A thanksgiving for your life and mine, finding each other mid-life and the love we shared for over 30 years.

Hope When the World Changes
1 Peter 1.3–9, 13; 2 Peter 3.13–18
First UMC, Kenosha (5/21/1995)

[Charlie]

... In 1889, when poet Walt Whitman was celebrating his 70th birthday, Mark Twain wrote him a letter:

> *You have lived the seventy years which are greatest in the world's history and richest in benefit and advancement to its peoples. What great births you have witnessed! The steamship, the railroad, the perfect cotton gin, the telegraphs, the phonograph, photogravure, the electrotype,*

the gaslight, the electric light, the sewing machine, and the amazing products of coal tar ... But wait thirty years, and then look out over the earth. You shall see marvels upon marvels added to those whose nativity you have witnessed...

And we *have* seen marvel after marvel as Twain predicted. ... For a moment or two last week, I was tempted to spend some time creating sentences that began, "I remember when ..." But why? And so what? There is not one of us here who is not affected by the rapid rate of change. And sometimes we rejoice at the changes we have experienced; but other times we feel powerless, hopeless and in a state of despair and disorientation. Change not only affects us, it afflicts us!

Hope when the world changes. How is hope sustained? For one thing, I believe we are called to uphold the past while remaining open to the future. Change gives birth to the illusion that we have nothing to learn from the past. But, you know, this has long been a human tendency. Twenty-six centuries ago the prophet Jeremiah faced a people who were experiencing rapid social change. And their accumulated wealth and wisdom led them to abandon the God of their ancestors.

... Now I'm grateful for our automatic washer and dryer, and my car, and the microwave; sometimes I'm grateful for the telephone; I'm certainly thankful for the newly created sulfa drugs which saved my life when I was four. But what about changing values, traditions, and beliefs? Sometimes they are being thrown out with brooms, buggies, and butter churns. Life is like ... maybe a box of chocolates, but I'd rather describe it as a relay race where you take what's handed to you, run the race that is set before you, and hand it on to the next generation.

... Hope in the midst of change is generated as we look back in thanksgiving at the heritage given to us and look ahead in gratitude and anticipation at those who will take what we give to them and carry it forward.

[Nancy]

Whoa. Changes? Not only have there been countless changes since you preached this—iPhones, Facebook, AI, and the pandemic—to name a few, but I've experienced several changes in the two years since you died. Two months after I bought the iPhone 13, the iPhone14 came out. The new person delivering the *New York Times* throws it at the garage door instead of the front, and our bank—my bank—merged with another and has a new name, color, (a weird chartreuse green) and Welcome, Welcome, Welcome signs that are splashed across the drive-up window.

I've changed, too. Another book *God's Human Future: The Struggle to Define Theology Today* is feeding my insatiable hunger to find and articulate a new theology. David Galston, the author, writes "We know, do we not, that God is a human creation? Language about God and religions concerning God are signs made to stand in place of the absence of God."

Can you see me smiling as I put these words into the iMac? I *love* this stuff.

Your sermon, of course, is about finding hope when the world changes. I'm finding hope that as the concept of God is changing within me, so are my feelings and thoughts about still being alive without you.

Charlie, I can't find anyone who cares about this topic or wants to read the books I'm excited about. Throughout our marriage you listened to my "way out" ideas without criticizing. But if you were alive, could we discuss Galston's chapter "Jesus the Teacher of Nothingness" during supper without an argument? Even if I baked your favorite stuffed porkchops and made sure you had a green vegetable?

A Letter to Cody
Galatians 3.26–29; 1 John 4.19; 1 Peter 2.4–5, 9–10
Belmont UMC, Belmont, MA (11/12/1995)

[Charlie]
Dear Cody,

This is an important day in your life. You are to be baptized, initiated into the Christian Church. And it is your grandfather who was ordained on June 10, 1962 by Bishop Hazen Werner and thus was given authority to administer the Sacraments, and who will have the privilege and responsibility of baptizing you.

For many years—even before your father was born—I have been collecting religious cartoons, so before I started writing this letter, I checked my baptism cartoons. I found three. Two are just silly. A pastor lifts the lid from the baptismal font and finds a goldfish swimming in the water. In another the minister says: "Mrs. Mott, I have never seen a child so well behaved at a baptism." And the mother replies, "Well, it's because my husband and I have been practicing on him with a watering can for a week."

In cartoon number three the pastor is ready to baptize the baby when a shark's fin appears above the water in the baptismal font. That may seem silly, too, but it reminded me that I never put my hand in the baptismal water casually; baptism is not something to be taken lightly; there needs to be caution exercised so that parents, sponsors, and the congregation understand what this act is all about. And so I'm writing this letter to you now so that when you can read you will understand how I felt about this day—what happened when I placed my wet hand on your head.

... Now the primary meaning of baptism is an announcement of God's love. You haven't earned God's love;

you are just 38 days old! ... Nevertheless, baptism is a promise that God makes to you now, saying, "I will never let you go. I will always love you."

... When your dad and two aunts had parakeets, I tried to get the birds to say the words, "John Wesley." It never happened! If they had learned to say "Wesley," then I was going to try to teach them to say "prevenient grace." That's right—if you know John Wesley, the next step is to know about prevenient grace. You see, that is what is being proclaimed when you and anyone else is baptized. It means that God's amazing grace love, is already active in your life.

[Nancy]
Charlie, I remember the gleam in your eyes and tears on your cheeks each time you baptized a grandchild. In this sermon addressed to Cody, you include scriptural references, membership in the church, and the responsibility of parents and the congregation to help him learn the Christian Story.

In 1995, a few drops of water on Cody's head promised the presence of *eternal love*. Eternal love was understood to be shown to Cody by the folks in the congregation, who promised support, encouragement, education, and spiritual formation. The vows taken on his behalf at baptism in the name of the Father, Son, and Holy Spirit, were also rituals of initiation into a world of creeds, doctrine, and dogma.

What happens to Cody and other baptized children who decide not to participate in the Christian Story? Are our grandchildren in worlds with stories that show them love as well as rules, expectations, and limitations?

Charlie, since your death I've been engrossed in the *history* of the Christian Story. The various ways the story is told today includes centuries of accumulated myths, many of which have been interpreted to dominate and oppress. I question religious terminology. I question how a human being ended up turning into a god. I question my role as a retired pastor. I read—and love—quotes like: *"If God is a human creation, good for us! We had to come up with something."* (Peter Schjeldahl) or, *"The trouble with the historical Jesus is that he was a poet. The form of his poetry was the artful and invocative parable, a product of his imagination."* (David Galston)

How would you respond to these quotes? Would you talk with me about the evolution of the idea of God? Aside from a couple friends who politely listen to me babble, folks who are interested in this stuff are rare. I miss you.

Forty years ago, when denominational judicatories asked why I wanted to go to seminary, I gave floaty, erudite, answers that must have included words from my credal indoctrination. When my friends asked, I answered, "I just want to get out of Appleton." They laughed, of course, but I was seeing myself baptizing babies and serving communion. Deep within and unsaid was my longing to be near holy things.

With the proper credentials and Holy Outfits, I began baptizing and serving communion. Naming and Nurturing. Our two sacraments. Among others, I baptized a grandson, a nephew, a mother and daughter, a dying 42-year-old non-churched woman, a baby named Jordan with Jordan River water I had just brought back from Israel, and two little girls from Africa, whose names I practiced for a week to be able to say correctly.

I served communion to the woman who was pissed with me because the piano was moved, a man with tobacco juice in his stubble, a child who spilled the cup of juice on the carpet, a transient who wanted to marry me, a wealthy member whose husband refused to take communion from a woman. My home church gave me a communion set, a hinged wooden box about the size of an Agatha Christie mystery, complete with a small covered container for bread cubes, a plastic bottle for juice, and four tiny glass cups, which I filled and took to hospitals, nursing homes, and shut-ins.

When did I catch on to the paradox? The closer I got to holy things, the more I learned about being human. *Being. Present. In the Moment.*

Charlie, though I'm having difficulty with the Christian Story, I have no difficulty believing in eternal love and I'm still growing in my ability to see its mystery. I cherish the stories that reveal it—like your anecdote about prevenient grace and the parakeet. I hadn't heard *that* story until I read this sermon.

Thank you.

Expect Joy
Luke 2.8–11; John 15.8–11;
Luke 24.52–53; 1 John 1.1–4
First UMC, Kenosha (12/26/1999)

[Charlie]

The reading of four scripture passages today was rather unusual, but I wanted to demonstrate how Joy—one of the fruits of the Spirit—is there throughout. The birth of Jesus brings forth a reason for joy...

As we close out this year, this century, this millennium, the newsmagazines and papers and television are filled with looks back at where we've been and predictions about the future. Now we can compile such lists of our own and concentrate on the frustration of life, the failures, the horrors of war, and be left with a sense of despair. Or we can create other lists and feel a sense of accomplishment and satisfaction that produces a sense of joy. Of course, if our joy is to be honest, it cannot be blind to human tragedy or indifferent to the world.

... Let's remember that the Apostle Paul writes so many of his statements about joy while in prison. "Rejoice in the Lord, always; again, I say, rejoice!" Obviously, joy can overcome life's suffering and tragedies. Joy is deep and lasting; it's not dependent upon emotions that we strive for. Joy is a gift!

... We could spend some time thinking about these occasions when we experienced joy in our lives, asking what were, what are the circumstances that brought, or bring joy forth. And, second, when joy fades, what kills it? There's not time to discuss both of these topics so I'm going to ask you to vote.

Nancy and I have been to plays, at least twice, in which the audience has voted their opinion about who the murderer was and the cast produced the appropriate ending from among several they were prepared to present. This morning you will get to choose the ending to this sermon. You will hear the ending the majority of you select. Ending number one will relate four ways that joy comes to us. Ending number two will talk about ways we kill joy that is present in others and in ourselves. One ending is a minute longer than the other, but I'm not going to tell you which one.

Are you ready to vote? If you want to have me talk about how joy comes to us, raise your hand. Now, if you want to hear ending number two and have me talk about ways we kill joy in our lives, raise your hand. Ending number ____ has it.

And to those of you who didn't vote, I hope it didn't mean you wanted me to stop right now ...?

[Nancy]
Very funny. Had I not been doing my thing at Bristol and Wesley Chapel that morning, I would have jumped up and

waved both my arms for the second ending. Having spent much of my life depressed, I want to know *how* and *why* I resist joy.

Did anyone raise their hand for you to stop? You didn't say. On the first page of the "killjoy" option, you wrote *not selected at any of the three services*. Nowhere did you print the vote counts.

I've promised myself to stop continuing these responses to your sermons by Thanksgiving and a few days ago I went through the last fifteen sermons I had saved. I rejected seven: Labor Day; Gambling; Second Coming; God is Tired; Gift of Patience; The Scandal of the Cross; and one which includes one of your limericks. Five of the eight left are variations on Speaking the Truth in Love, which I will leave for last.

Initially, I chose to include this sermon on Joy without reading it carefully because it was another example of your creativity. Today, I read the whole thing. During the first ending, you summarize that joy is basically a gift, and, because it's Christmas, you proclaim the unexpected birth of Jesus as a joyous gift. Though you mentioned a couple destructive messages we give ourselves to "kill joy," (I'm not good enough. I don't deserve it. I've made mistakes.) you address most of the second ending dealing with put-downs within church interactions.

Neither of your endings helped. If joy is a gift, as your sermon title indicates, I have to look for it or expect it. I expected joy a few weeks ago when I got an invitation to Martha's 100th birthday open house. Several attempts at arrangements to get to Appleton to be present at the celebration of one of our former secretaries didn't work out, but three days after her party, my son, Steve, drove me to her home.

We arrived at noon. Her daughter, Ruth, met us at the door.

"We just brought her home from the hospital," Ruth said.
"Oh. I don't want to intrude, I ..."

"No," Ruth interrupted. "She knew you were coming and has been waiting. She wants to see you."

While still in the hallway, I could see Martha lying covered up to her chin in white blankets. In the bedroom, Steve, a paramedic, helped Ruth and another daughter, Mary, adjust the oxygen tank and then the three of them left Martha and me alone.

Charlie, I want to believe you were with Martha and me as we laughed, cried, sang old hymns, and remembered back 40 years to church people and staff and the gentle jokes you played on each other.

"You were the perfect secretary," I said.

"No one is perfect." Thin, clear, oxygen tubes framed Martha's smile.

"Well, okay. You are a 99," I countered. She squeezed my hand.

The impending arrival of a person to admit Martha to Hospice, prompted my leaving. I kissed her forehead, said goodbye, and joined my son and Martha's daughters in the living room.

Oh Charlie. Martha died a few hours after I left. I'm still struck and stuck with how, why, who and what questions to ask the universe about the timing of my visit. Questions that will never be answered.

Charlie. Martha's memorial service is today. I am not there. I am here alone. 110 miles away, trying to find the joy you preached about. Was my half-hour with Martha joy? I cry while I write this. I say I can't do this, can't do this, can't do this. Do I want to stop these conversations with you to avoid more sorrow?

And, Charlie, what prompted me to slide my chair away from the keyboard and look out the window to see a clear blue sky with an unseasonably warm November sun shining on maple leaves dancing burnt orange in a gentle breeze? You say joy is a gift. Was that fleeting moment of contentment I felt a gift? Was it joy?

The Scandal of the Cross
1 Corinthians 1.18-31
First UMC, Kenosha (4/4/1992)

[Charlie]

A few of you may have been at the 10:15 service of worship on December 19 this past year. If so, you'll remember that I had the opportunity to baptize my two grandchildren. The day before, Nancy told me that she wanted to buy small gold crosses for the girls to wear, and so we went shopping. I didn't know there were so many sizes and choices, and I'm sure that the clerks who waited on us must have thought us irreverent from the comments we made about some of the crosses. You see, ministers don't usually buy crosses; people give them to us as presents. In fact, my wife recently brought home a cross made out of white chocolate that someone had created. We both hesitated to bite into it. Today I brought along with me the only two crosses that I think I've ever bought for myself. The first came from Bolivia and is made out of a special wood that has these holes in it—it is truly a "holy" cross. The other one I found in a bookstore in Weston, Vermont at a Catholic retreat center I visited and it holds a great fascination for me.

The cross. Who would have thought that this means of primitive torture would become an object of art, on sale in jewelry stores and bookstores, made into chocolate and displayed in our churches. Paul called the cross a scandal, and some people, otherwise sympathetic with Christianity, are embarrassed by the cross; they certainly do not know what to make of it.

[Nancy]
Well, Charlie, I don't know what to make of the cross either. I don't wear one. And, I wouldn't buy one now, especially for a grandchild's baptism. Of course, the Apostle Paul, in his letter to the church at Corinth described the cross as a horrifying, humiliating scandal to many, but he was writing to people who were responding to an undefeated power of love they had seen in Jesus. Good news then.

Does the cross mean good news now? There's the trouble I'm having, sweetheart. I intended to skip commenting on this sermon. I changed my mind after a discussion in the adult Sunday School class yesterday.

"Jesus died for me," one woman said. "He saved me."

"Saved you from what?" I asked.

I really didn't want to get into the discussion that followed about sin and forgiveness and Jesus having to die so that we could get into heaven.

"No," I said, when someone asked me to comment. "I can't. I can't go there."

Of course, I did. I went there. Loudly.

"I can't do atonement theology anymore," I hollered. "It makes me helpless. I have to count on Jesus to do 'it' for me, whatever 'it' is. I have no agency of my own." Somewhere in my rant I said, "I've been part of a story for 17 centuries that focuses on sin instead of the goodness of love's life-giving power."

I said, "I don't take communion. I read about the evolution of the idea of God. I don't fit in! I don't even know who the fuck I am anymore!"

I don't remember who broke the awkward silence or what was said, but the class went on. I went on, too. I didn't try to explain myself. What I had said was true.

Charlie, I'm changing. I don't know who I am.

I came home and made a list of who I think I am:
- Retired clergywoman
- Writer

Surprisingly, until now I didn't think of friend, mother, grandmother, and great-grandmother. Each one of these roles is relational and I spend most of my days alone.

Wrestling With God
Genesis 32.22–32
Wauwatosa Avenue UMC (7/31/2010)

[Charlie]

Pastor Sue has been preaching about Jacob for the past three weeks. You've discovered that Jacob was a crook, a cheat, and a manipulator who found a way to twist every situation to his own advantage. Frederick Buechner describes him as a man who was never satisfied. "He wanted the moon, and if he'd ever managed to bilk Heaven out of that, he would have been back the next morning for the stars to go with it."

Having cheated his brother of his birthright and his father of his blessing, Jacob runs away, far away to work for his uncle, Laban. ...After twenty years, Jacob ends up owning just about everything that isn't tied down on Uncle Laban's farm. But then God instructs Jacob, "Go back to the land of your fathers. And know that I will be with you."

Go back? This meant Jacob would have to deal with his past. He would have to reckon with his brother, Esau, who had threatened to kill him. He would have to face his father, Isaac, whom he had deceived. He would be forced to come to grips with all that he had been.

Well, he decides to obey the Divine Voice and trust God's command no matter how great the danger. So, he begins his journey home. As he nears home he sends messengers ahead and follows up with gifts: 220 goats; 220 sheep; 30 camels; 50 cows and bulls; and 30 donkeys. The verse just before today's reading says: "Jacob hopes the gifts would make Esau friendly, so Esau would be glad to see him when they met."

Now we come to the strangest part of the story ... Today's Scripture ...

[Nancy]

Ah. The scripture was the story of Jacob's wrestling though the night with a "man." Jacob will not let go of his combatant. He wants the man's name. Morning comes. The foe does not divulge an identity, but rather gives Jacob a new name—Israel. In addition to a name that symbolizes a nation, the stranger leaves Jacob with a limp. Scripture reports Jacob decided he was wrestling with God.

I've always liked this story and can definitely identify with wrestling. These days I'm aware of an inner struggle with an unnamed adversary. Oh, names have shown up dozens of times throughout my life. God. Jesus. Holy One. Sophia. Mary With No Mouth. Wise Old Woman. Divine Source. Mystery. Once years ago, it appeared as a bubble wearing a fedora. What was *that* about?

Charlie, I love that you used the name Divine Voice. Over the years, you had clearly expanded your image of God. For a few weeks now, I've addressed the presence within me as

Beloved Guest, but I know that the "thing" with which I tussle is ultimately nameless.

I think of the quote of St. Ephrem the Syrian: *Blessed is he (or she or they) who has appeared to our human race under so many metaphors*. The word Jesus is another metaphor that no longer feels like a pebble in my shoe.

But Charlie, your sermon focused less on the name of Jacob's opponent and more on his relationship with his brother, Esau. Jacob had to reckon—wrestle—with past behaviors that had damaged the relationship with his brother before he could ask forgiveness and hope for reconciliation.

You challenge folks to wrestle with their personal behaviors which cause damage in relationships. And, as we were taught in homiletics, you make sure the Good News of a loving and forgiving God is present. However, some of the people with whom I want reconciliation are metaphor challenged and some are dead. I find the process difficult to manage.

I'm still alive.

Today I'm wrestling about who to include for Thanksgiving, what to do with the nasty yellow warning sign on my computer screen about apps, and how much money to send to the latest Planned Parenthood request.

I'll add your challenge to my list.

Until Death Do Us Part
Matthew 19.1–9
First UMC, Kenosha (8/8/1993)

[Charlie]
    I sat at my typewriter staring out the window last week for a very long time composing in my head many introductory paragraphs for this sermon. None seemed satisfactory until I decided to say this: "I have been divorced." Many, but not all, of you know that. The legal divorce took place over five years ago when I lived in Appleton. But the *actual* divorce—the marriage failure and emotional divorce—occurred several years before that. Still, the last time I preached on this passage from Matthew that I just read to you was eleven years ago and I was not divorced then.

    As I reread that old sermon last week, I was pleasantly surprised at many of my insights and the development of the text; yet there was a missing element—most of what I said was second-hand stuff and was perhaps a tad judgmental. No longer!

    Let's begin with a few statistics …

    … Now the purpose of the statistics and the explanations for *some* of today's divorces was to set the stage for an examination of Jesus' words on the subject of divorce. Millions today are asking the same or similar questions that the Pharisees asked Jesus: "Is it lawful for a man to divorce his wife for any cause?"

    In order to understand Jesus' response we need to be familiar with the context of his words. At that time—the first century—women were viewed as property and were completely at the disposal of their fathers or husbands. A divorce paper could be written out in a minute before two witnesses, and the woman had to leave. The husband did have to return the dowry, but that was all! ...

A second thing that helps us understand the context for Jesus' words is the fact that there was quite a debate going on among Jewish scholars of that time. You see, the whole matter of divorce and remarriage rested on one brief passage in Deuteronomy. It said that when a man found some indecency in his wife he could divorce her. But what was this indecency? The strict conservative scholars defined "some indecency" as meaning unfaithfulness and nothing else.

A school of liberal scholars defined "indecency" in the widest possible way—almost anything a wife did was grounds for divorce: if she spoiled her husband's dinner by burning it or by putting in too much salt; if she went out with her head uncovered; if she was childless; if she talked with men in the streets; if she spoke disrespectfully of his parents. Out! And now the Pharisees want to know where Jesus stands on this issue— Are you a liberal or a conservative?

In his response Jesus, as he so often did, went behind the law itself to the intention of God—the ideal of creation. The statement in Deuteronomy permitting divorce in some circumstances was God's accommodation to human failure and sin, but the ideal according to Jesus is found in Genesis: "The two become one." As on other occasions, Jesus moved away from a law intended to deal with a specific situation and he establishes a principle of life; namely that marriage is intended to bring people together for life in a relationship of trust and commitment that should never be broken!

[Nancy]

Well. Touchy subject. I found one of your half-sheets with a statement you read *before* the service even started:

> *In today's service we will be responding to a request to preach on the question the Pharisees asked Jesus: "Is it lawful for a man to divorce his wife for any cause?" A stanza from the second hymn we will sing today sets the theme for my response to that question:*
>> *When love is torn and trust betrayed,*
>>> *pray strength to love till torments fade;*
>> *till lovers keep no score of wrong,*
>>> *but hear through pain love's Easter song.*

Charlie, I resisted even reading this sermon. I didn't know how to respond without tapping into the pain of my first marriage. Interestingly enough, the last seminary course I took included the rabbinical argument to which you referred. I wrote a twelve-page paper that compared divorce—then and now. Though still in my first marriage, I slanted the paper toward absolving partners of their "until death do us part" vows. Was I trying to forgive myself two years before the divorce?

With this sensitive topic, you cite statistics, list reasons for divorce, and then spend several pages describing how Jesus often responded to his detractors by moving away from the law, which was intended to deal with a specific situation, toward establishing a principle of life.

Near your conclusion you quote part of the United Methodist Social Principles:

> *... where marriage partners, even after thoughtful consideration and counsel, are estranged beyond reconciliation, we recognize divorce as regrettable, but recognize the right of divorced persons to remarry ...*

You end with a prayer from *The Book of Worship*.

Keeping this sermon and now responding to it evokes memories of our marriage. Only once—very early—was the word "divorce" said aloud. I don't remember the issue, which had to have been heated. You were in the kitchen and shouted,

"Divorce?" as if splitting was an option to consider. I was standing in the dining room by the table, simultaneously stunned by your comment and aware of a strong, silent "No!" Somehow, we resolved that argument and many more.

Until death parted us.

Now, doing these sermons... if I keep my promise to finish by Thanksgiving Day, what will it mean? Will it mean I'm saying another good bye to you? I cry when I envision another parting.

Speaking the Truth in Love
Ephesians 4.1–3, 14–16
First UMC, Appleton (6/11/1989)

[Charlie]

"United Methodist ministers get moved too often." I've heard that said on several occasions during the past two months. That's certainly better to hear than "You didn't move soon enough." As it turned out, I've been in Appleton for seven-and-a-half years.

That means, of course, that there are a lot of you here today who were not here on January 31, 1982 when I stood up to preach. I was nervous, anxious, grieving the loss of people I knew so well in Oconomowoc. But I was also filled with a sense of anticipation and excitement. How many of you were present the first Sunday I preached here? Would you raise your hands?

I want to go back to that first sermon and review some of the things I said then. It was called "Speaking the Truth in Love" —the same title as today's message. That text from Ephesians expresses what I attempted in my ministry among you: "By speaking the truth in a spirit of love, we must grow up in every way to Christ."

I made some promises to you in that sermon...

These are the aspects of the gospel I've tried to present ...

I certainly hope that these years we have had together have been marked by growth on your part—spiritual growth—as you have heard me attempt to speak the truth in love. And I'm grateful for that affirming word spoken and written which I have received throughout my ministry here: such communication has been especially important during these past two months as we say goodbye to each other.

Now I want to relate some of the key things I believe I've learned during these 7½ years with you. For one thing, various life experiences have led me to ever greater levels of understanding and empathy with many of you. I now know what it is to have to use glasses; I had a brief, mild case of shingles that left me shuddering at the thought of what a severe case might be like; my father died of cancer and my only uncle died as well—cutting me off from the past at the very time I wanted to know more about traditions and family history; my brother-in-law committed suicide; my three children have all graduated from college and are on their own with their relationship with Dad—now based solely upon love and concern, not food and finances; there was counseling I participated in surrounding some events and behaviors involving one of my children; and there was the pain and trauma associated with a failed marriage. As a young pastor I used to marvel at the wisdom and understanding of some of my older colleagues. Now I recognize the price that is paid for some of that first-hand experience, but ultimately the pastor and the people benefit and learn from it, I believe.

Second, I continue to grow in my ability to enjoy the gift of life as it is given each day ... I'm living much more in the present moment than I once did, and I'm a bit closer to the anxiety-free peace and life that Jesus commended, than I once was.

Third, I've learned to admit my vulnerability to others much more so than I once could. Deep down I always knew my humanness and failings, but I seldom let others into that part of myself. And the times I cried as an adult could be counted on one hand. Now, I cry at movies and more importantly, I can cry with and for others and can share much more readily who I am.

There is so much more, but I'll conclude with this fourth area of growth and discovery: the freeing, liberating, exciting power of Christianity. In Galatians the Apostle Paul wrote, "This life I live now, I live by faith in the Son of God, who loved me and gave his life for me." That's how I feel and it certainly helps account for the joy I feel and the enthusiasm I usually express.

Someone has said, "If we are not enjoying our religion, something must be wrong with it." I agree. We gather to celebrate life—the temporary life we have here on earth and the eternal life which is also ours.

So in what we do here in worship and in what we do out there beyond these walls, let us express the joy and excitement of people who have been challenged by Christ the Disturber, who have been restored by Christ the Healer, and who have made a commitment to Christ as Master and Savior.

Goodbye!

[Nancy]
Charlie. I began these pages with your "hello" sermon in Appleton and chose this Appleton "goodbye" sermon as a fitting Book-End.

Today is November 26, 2022. Two days after Thanksgiving. I'm having trouble ending these conversations with you. I cry. Will I continue to be in touch with you? How?

A few weeks ago, I promised myself to finish by Thanksgiving. (I'm almost there) Because you died during Covid, the remembrance was confined to a few minutes during an outdoor Sunday worship service, and I wanted to provide a written celebration of your life. Paragraphs I chose from your sermons gave me the perfect means by which to describe the way I knew you and also give you another chance to be heard.

Responding to these selected sermons has been a way for me to feel you close. Over the years of our marriage, I've heard stories about you from your children, former parishioners, and colleagues, but your earlier sermons, which I had never read, gave me additional glimpses of who you were.

While reading and rereading, I saw you grow: Your tendency to be judgmental softened to compassion; you began to relax and enjoy time off from the 24/7 work; and you more easily and readily shared your feelings. I was reminded of the Bible verse you said was your favorite: *If we live, we live to the Lord, and if we die, we die to the Lord, so then whether we live or whether we die, we are the Lord's* (Romans 14.8). I experienced you as living day after day out of this belief.

Though I've gone through piles of Kleenex, this process has been healing for me. The wrenching memories of those last four months of your life have moved over to allow delightful and blissful moments we shared to appear: the balloon ride; Dickey's Cay; Paragon Pinball. Your absence is palpable. Yet, I'm not only learning to survive without you, I'm growing. And surprisingly to me, I'm growing in my faith.

Toward the end of your hello and goodbye sermons, you repeated and agreed with this quote: *Someone has said, "If we are not enjoying our religion, something must be wrong with it."*

For years I've thought something was wrong with our religion. Since your death, through books, webinars, and conversations, I'm beginning to understand what is wrong. You found joy and excitement at "living in the Lord." I'm finding joy and excitement as I understand—for me—what is wrong and to see ways to change it. While your "living in the Lord" worked well for you, one of the things I'm finding wrong with our religion are the words.

Like Lord.

Yesterday, when I turned on the tv, the last half hour of the 1943 movie "Lassie Come Home" was on. There was Edmund Gwen, Elsa Lanchester, and a 12-year-old Elizabeth Taylor. How many times has that movie been satirized? How many times have I laughed at jokes and cartoons about Timmy in the well? Yet, I was captivated clear to the end and sobbed as Lassie and the boy, played by Roddy McDowell, were reunited.

That 80-year-old movie reveals again the deep human need for connections through love. I learned to love and be loved by and with you. Your words through these sermons have helped to reawaken a longing for me to be reconnected with my truer self—a presence, whose name is elusive.

What a gift you have given me. Thank You.

I cry now as I say this goodbye to you. I have no idea if we will ever be together again, but as I learn new ways to be with me, I trust I will discover new ways to be with you.

I will always love you,

Nancy

Made in the USA
Monee, IL
26 March 2023